D1032228

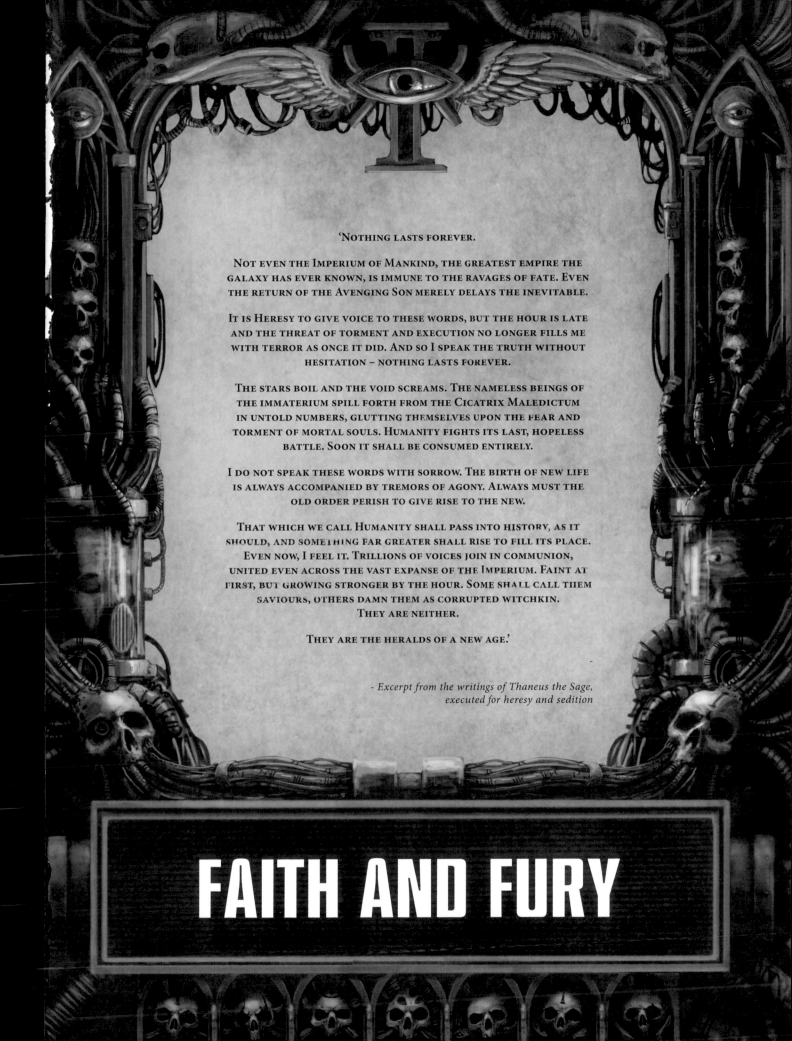

'Nothing lasts forever.

Not even the Imperium of Mankind, the greatest empire the galaxy has ever known, is immune to the ravages of fate. Even the return of the Avenging Son merely delays the inevitable.

It is Heresy to give voice to these words, but the hour is late and the threat of torment and execution no longer fills me with terror as once it did. And so I speak the truth without hesitation – nothing lasts forever.

The stars boil and the void screams. The nameless beings of the immaterium spill forth from the Cicatrix Maledictum in untold numbers, glutting themselves upon the fear and torment of mortal souls. Humanity fights its last, hopeless battle. Soon it shall be consumed entirely.

I do not speak these words with sorrow. The birth of new life is always accompanied by tremors of agony. Always must the old order perish to give rise to the new.

That which we call Humanity shall pass into history, as it should, and something far greater shall rise to fill its place. Even now, I feel it. Trillions of voices join in communion, united even across the vast expanse of the Imperium. Faint at first, but growing stronger by the hour. Some shall call them saviours, others damn them as corrupted witchkin.
They are neither.

They are the heralds of a new age.'

- Excerpt from the writings of Thaneus the Sage,
executed for heresy and sedition

FAITH AND FURY

CONTENTS

PRODUCED BY GAMES WORKSHOP IN NOTTINGHAM

With thanks to the Mournival and the Infinity Circuit for their additional playtesting services

Psychic Awakening: Faith and Fury © Copyright Games Workshop Limited 2019. Psychic Awakening: Faith and Fury, GW, Games Workshop, Space Marine, 40K, Warhammer, Warhammer 40,000, the 'Aquila' Double-headed Eagle logo, and all associated logos, illustrations, images, names, creatures, races, vehicles, locations, weapons, characters, and the distinctive likenesses thereof, are either ® or TM, and/or © Games Workshop Limited, variably registered around the world. All Rights Reserved.

No part of this publication may be reproduced, stored in a retrieval system, or transmitted in any form or by any means, electronic, mechanical, photocopying, recording or otherwise, without the prior permission of the publishers.

This is a work of fiction. All the characters and events portrayed in this book are fictional, and any resemblance to real people or incidents is purely coincidental. British Cataloguing-in-Publication Data. A catalogue record for this book is available from the British Library. Pictures used for illustrative purposes only.

Certain Citadel products may be dangerous if used incorrectly and Games Workshop does not recommend them for use by children under the age of 16 without adult supervision. Whatever your age, be careful when using glues, bladed equipment and sprays and make sure that you read and follow the instructions on the packaging.

Games Workshop Limited, Willow Rd, Lenton, Nottingham, NG7 2WS

games-workshop.com

INTRODUCTION

The galaxy is in turmoil. Fully half of the Imperium of Mankind is engulfed in darkness and terror, and the forces of the Dark Gods rampage across Humanity's domain. In the Talledus System, a ferocious war rages between the ranks of the God-Emperor and the servants of the Ruinous Powers.

The immense warp storm known as the Cicatrix Maledictum has carved the Imperium in two. Humanity's defenders – including the mighty Space Marines of the Adeptus Astartes – find themselves assailed on all fronts, desperately attempting to fend off the onslaught of the servants of Chaos and opportunistic xenos raiders. Even amidst the heartlands of the Emperor's realm, close to Holy Terra itself, anarchy and terror reign. The traitorous warlords of the Heretic Astartes launch their hate-fuelled crusades with impunity, aiming to tear apart the Imperium they once served and spread the insidious worship of the Dark Gods amongst the terrified populace.

The Talledus System is one such ravaged domain, a once-shining stronghold of the Imperial creed now transformed into a war zone contested by the worshippers of the Emperor of Mankind and those sworn to the Chaos Pantheon. As this war of faith grows ever-more bloody and brutal, the psychic trauma generated by the Cicatrix Maledictum gives rise to miracles and psychic manifestations of unrivalled scale and power. To some, these bizarre and terrifying occurrences are yet further proof that the galaxy is approaching its inevitable final hour of doom. To others, these events are proof of the God-Emperor's divine will, actualised through his loyal servants.

Whatever the truth of it, this surge of empyric disruption will unravel the tapestry of the 41st Millennium forever, giving rise to a new era of psychic awakening.

IN THIS BOOK

This book is part of Psychic Awakening, an ongoing series set after the Great Rift splits the galaxy. It contains an overview from the perspective of the Space Marines, the elite champions of Humanity, and their hated nemeses – the Heretic Astartes.

Inside you will find:

- The tale of the war for the Talledus System, a furious conflict of faith.
- Theatres of War and missions to echo the Faith and Fury storyline.
- Additional rules for Space Marines armies, including updated datasheets, Relics and more for the Black Templars Chapter.
- A suite of rules and a name generator table for six Traitor Legions of the Heretic Astartes.

FAITH UNBOUND

The time of the Great Rift found the Imperium reeling, assailed on a million fronts by the surging forces of Chaos. It was only the return of the Primarch Roboute Guilliman and the fury of the Primaris Space Marines that held back the tide. At this dark hour, the power of faith would offer Humanity the faintest glimmer of hope.

The Indomitus Crusade swept forth from Terra with furious purpose, driving the forces of Chaos before them and bringing hope to hundreds of besieged worlds. None but the Primarch of the Ultramarines could have overseen such a decisive counter-attack. To those whom he commanded, it seemed that Roboute Guilliman did not rest for a moment. No sooner had one victory been achieved than he began to lay the foundations of the next. The crusade's momentum could not slow, for that might allow the heretical forces an opportunity to regroup.

So it was that as the crusade ventured deeper and deeper into occupied territory, pushing into regions ravaged by daemonic hordes and migrating xenos fleets, those territories in their wake were left to manage as best they could. The threats they faced were many. In the aftermath of the Great Rift the entire galaxy was stricken by nightmarish phenomena, temporal disruption and terrible warp storms. It was the Imperium Nihilus – those regions that lay beyond the line of the Great Rift – that suffered the worst of these occurrences, but nowhere in the Imperium of Mankind was left unscarred. Even across the gleaming sanctuary worlds of the Segmentum Solar, horror struck. Isolated warp storms tore through unprepared systems, swallowing battlefleets and spilling daemonic entities across the surface of worlds. Such was the anarchic disruption of reality that Chaos armadas, Ork raiding fleets and other deadly xenos forces were carried vast distances across the tides of the warp and vomited back into realspace on the far side of the galaxy.

Worse still, the predations of the Great Enemy intensified. Like slavering wolves, the Heretic Astartes and their allies struck at the underbelly of the Imperium, emerging from the roiling stars to raid and pillage across the Segmentum Solar. Many of these incursions were directionless and savage, little more than the servants of Chaos indulging their base desires for blood and slaughter. Yet they masked a greater plan, overseen by those who served the will of the Dark Gods with a far more insidious agenda. The Word Bearers sought to spread their heretic faith into the very heart of Humanity's domain. The sons of Lorgar had foreseen a struggle not only for the territory of the Imperium, but its very spirit. The souls of mortals were the currency over which this war of faith would be fought.

Allying with fellow Traitor Legions, such as the piratical reavers of the Night Lords and the relentless Iron Warriors, the Word Bearers sought to spread fear and hopelessness far and wide. Through dark ritual, system-wide sacrifice and terror tactics, they intensified the power of Chaos, hoping to break the will of the Imperium's mortal populace. Those who accepted the primacy of the Dark Gods were spared – their collective damnation empowering the spread of corruption.

blind to the subtle, hexagrammatic patterns of the Word Bearers' rituals, Imperial forces failed to recognise either the disaster building behind their lines, or the rampant spread of panic and heresy. Planet by planet, the shadow of Chaos spread.

Only the Sisters of Battle, the zealous warrior-champions of the Imperial Creed, foresaw this deadly threat. Many a Canoness of the Adepta Sororitas witnessed the same apocalyptic visions: maws of utter blackness stretching wide to devour the light of the faithful, twin-headed aquilas torn apart by hungering shadows, and stars drowned in the blood of innocents. The holy orders of the Sisterhood could not spread word of the horror they had uncovered, for across the galaxy astropathic communications were drowned out by warp-screams and the howling static of daemonic entities. Word would have to be delivered in person. Thus it was

that the Orders Militant of the Adepta Sororitas dispatched their battlefleets in greater numbers than ever before, guided by the visions granted by their beloved God-Emperor.

Even as the Sisters of Battle brought hope and fierce defiance to scores of war-ravaged worlds, it seemed certain that the Word Bearers' plans would come to fruition. Yet the sons of Lorgar had not counted upon the new and dramatic phenomenon that began to manifest across those contested planets. The immense eruption of psychic energy unleashed by the Cicatrix Maledictum gave rise not only to

warp-spawned nightmares, but acts of faith and wondrous miracles on a scale unheard of. Humble, mortal worshippers of the God-Emperor bore witness to manifestations of the Emperor Angelic, flocks of golden eagles and columns of scintillating flame that seared daemonic and heretic flesh alike. These miracles galvanised those who bore witness to them, firming their resolve and filling their hearts with defiance even in the face of the horrors unleashed against them. So began a great war of faith that set the dark prophets of the Heretic Astartes against the acts of hope and belief inspired by the Sisters of Battle and their allies.

TALLEDUS

For ten thousand years the sanctified Talledus System shone as a beacon of Humanity's might. A realm of glittering shrine worlds populated by billions of pious servants of the God-Emperor, its glory seemed eternal and untarnishable.

The Talledus System lay in the centre of the Veritus Sub-sector, a region of space replete with Imperial worlds and navigable warp routes. It was seen as a stronghold of the Ecclesiarchy, a vibrant symbol of the Imperial Creed's galaxy-spanning influence and power. Its capital world of Benediction was entirely covered by a golden theocropolis of astonishing scale, the entirety of the planet's surface reshaped and sculpted into a mausoleum-temple to house the corpses of thousands of saints.

Many faithful pilgrims of the God-Emperor would gladly have given their lives just to see the spire-mountains of Lux Eternis, to walk amidst the statues of long-dead priests and hierophants, to hear the sound of psalms echoing through the artificial valleys and stained-glass towers of the Grand Honorificum.

This ambitious project was started by none other than the legendary Ecclesiarch Sebastian Thor. During the 36th Millennium, Thor led a great revolt against the depravities of his predecessor, Ecclesiarch and High Lord Goge Vandire. Thoroughly insane and murderous, Vandire had become convinced that he alone was the God-Emperor's divine instrument and successor. Anyone who questioned his increasingly deranged pronouncements was subject to hideous torture, then a summary execution at the hands of the Daughters of the Emperor, a sect of pious warriors that had been swayed into Vandire's service.

The Talledus System suffered terribly during those dark days. Its governor, Hectus Carmine, was one of the first to openly and publicly decry the outrages of Goge Vandire. In doing so he earned the mad Ecclesiarch's fury. Carmine's home world of Talledus was invaded by forces loyal to Vandire, who were faced with the governor's steadfast Astra

Militarum regiments and thousands of the God-Emperor's faithful who refused to acknowledge Vandire's rule. After a fierce conflict that raged for many months, Carmine and hundreds of his co-conspirators were finally captured and put on trial. The deposed governor was brutalised publicly for more than a month and ultimately burned alive on the steps of his palatial residence, while his populace was forced to witness. Not content with this blood price, Vandire ordered a grand purge of heretics across the sub-sector. On worlds such as Boras Minor, Ghreddask and Satropol, the measures taken by the insane Ecclesiarch would live in infamy. Once a prosperous system famed for its splendour, Talledus was reduced to a shadow of its former glory.

Sebastian Thor was the leader of the Confederation of Light, an alliance of faithful souls determined to end Vandire's time as Ecclesiarch, which had come to be known as the Reign of Blood. Thor gathered his forces – which included several Space Marine Chapter Masters – to Holy Terra, where they overthrew the tyrant and his loyal servants. In the process, Thor revealed the depths of Vandire's heresy to the Daughters of the Emperor, who repaid their master's lies with the edge of a power sword. As Vandire's severed head struck the floor of his chamber, the terror that had enveloped the Imperium was

'Ten thousand blessed saints rest eternal amidst the silent halls of Benediction. It is a world steeped in the blood of the faithful.'

*- Canoness Arkasia
Fury of the Order of the
Ebon Chalice*

finally ended. In the aftermath of this bloody coup, Thor - having convinced the High Lords of Terra of the righteousness of his actions - was chosen to become the new Ecclesiarch.

Thor was a bold and determined reformer. He decreed that the Daughters of the Emperor, having shown their true loyalty, would become the Chamber Militant of the Ecclesiarchy – renamed the Sisters of Battle, they would faithfully serve the will of the God-Emperor. Having put in place measures to ensure that an event as disastrous as Vandire's Reign of Blood could not occur again, Thor departed Terra and began a grand tour of the Imperium's holy sites. One of the first sub-sectors the new Ecclesiarch visited was Veritus, and its broken capital of Talledus was his first port of call.

Though they had suffered greatly at the hands of the church, the survivors of Vandire's purges greeted their new Ecclesiarch reverently when he visited the ruins of Talledus. Moved by their faith, Thor ordered the construction of a grand monument to Hectus Carmine and all who had lost their lives during the Reign of Blood. The limitless coffers of the Ecclesiarchy were opened, and upon the ashes of the past were fashioned soaring temples and mausoleum-cities of gold. Thor decreed that Talledus be renamed Benediction in honour of the fallen.

Over the following centuries the power and influence of the Veritus Sub-sector grew unchecked. The immense wealth generated by sacred tithes, pilgrimage tolls and the generous offerings of the God-Emperor's faithful flowed back into the vaults of the Ecclesiarchy.

In order to protect this valuable and imposing symbol of their power, Thor's successors ensured that several fortress-sanctuaries of the Sisters of Battle were built upon Martyr's Rest and its neighbouring

worlds. Entire Astra Militarum regiments were diverted to protect its borders, and the Ecclesiarchy's tithe-collectors roamed the space lanes of the Veritus Sub-sector, ensuring that the God-Emperor's due was paid in full. The dockyards at Satrapol were amongst the largest in the Imperium. Thousands upon thousands of vessels were packed together in cramped mooring claws, kept stationary for months and sometimes even years as the Ecclesiarchy's agents methodically ensured that every tithe was collected. Those who failed to pay what was owed, or in any way roused the ire of the church, were dealt with by the ruthlessly zealous Ghreddask Illuminators. These crack Astra Militarum regiments did not technically answer to the Adeptus Ministorum, as the Decree Passive, passed in the aftermath of the Reign of Blood, prevented

the church from maintaining such a military body ever again. Yet, such was the ferocity of their faith, the Illuminators maintained suspiciously close ties with members of the Talledoran priesthood.

So did Talledus thrive for thousands of years. Even when the Great Rift tore open and Terra itself was savaged by the daemonic hordes of the Dark Gods, the Veritus Sub-sector remained untouched. The prophets of Benediction claimed that the faithful of Talledus lived under the eternal protection of the God-Emperor, a reward for all that they had suffered.

Such predictions would prove utterly false. The Dark Gods had set their eyes upon this gleaming jewel in Humanity's crown, and their greatest mortal champions planned to see it burn in the fires of Chaos.

BATTLEGROUND OF FAITH

The small yet incredibly influential sub-sector of Veritus lies near to the centre of Segmentum Solar. For centuries a prosperous bastion of the Imperial faith, ever since the opening of the Cicatrix Maledictum and the subsequent resurgence of Chaos forces it has become the location of a bitter and bloody struggle for the souls of its mortal inhabitants.

NAOGEDDON

DIMMAMAR

STORM OF THE EMPEROR'S WRATH

HALO STARS

SEGMENTUM OBSCURUS

FINIAL SECTOR

CALIXIS SECTOR

CYPRA MUNDI

VALHALLA

MORDIAN

ALARIC

THE EYE OF TERROR

VIGILUS

CADIA   BELIS CORONA   PISCINA

CHINCHARE

NECRON MEPHRIT DYNASTY

AGRIPINAA   NACHMUND GAUNTLET

MOLOV

HYDRAPHUR

ARMAGEDDON   ELYSIA

CICATRIX MALEDICTUM

SEGMENTUM SOLAR

LASTRATI

GOLGOTHA

VORDRAST

SEGMENTUM PACIFICUS

TERRA & MARS

RYZA

THE MAELSTROM

CATACHAN

GATHALAMOR

NECROMUNDA

MACHARIA

BADAB

ULTIMA MACHARIA

KRIEG   LUTHER MCINTYRE

CHIROS

TALLARN

UHULIS SECTOR

OPHELIA

NOCTURNE   BALOR

V'RUN

SIREN'S STORM

ALEUSIS

BANE'S LANDING

SOLSTICE

RYNN'S WORLD

NEPHILIM SECTOR

SEGMENTUM TEMPESTUS

REDUCTUS SECTOR

AGRAX

BAKKA   ANTAGONIS

GRYPHONNE IV

SAN LEOR

ILLUSTRIS   THE VEILED REGION

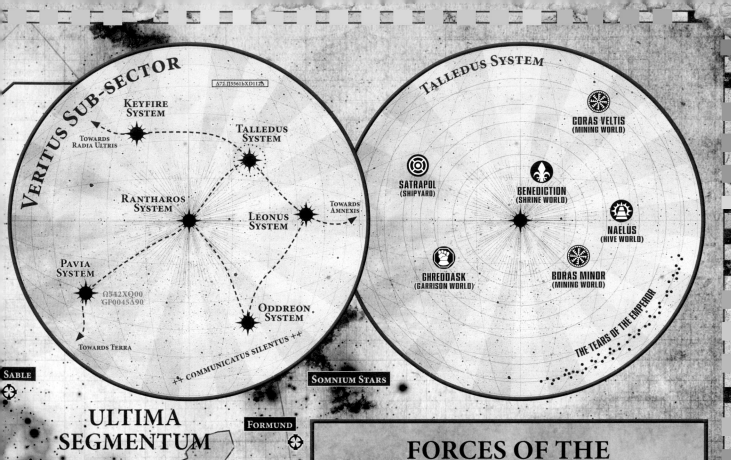

VERITUS SUB-SECTOR

Δ72.JI5561bXD112

KEYFIRE SYSTEM

Towards Radia Ultris

TALLEDUS SYSTEM

RANTHAROS SYSTEM

LEONUS SYSTEM

Towards Amnexis

PAVIA SYSTEM

Ω542XQ00
GP0045Δ90

ODDREON SYSTEM

Towards Terra

++ COMMUNICATUS SILENTUS ++

TALLEDUS SYSTEM

CORAS VELTIS (MINING WORLD)

SATRAPOL (SHIPYARD)

BENEDICTION (SHRINE WORLD)

NAELUS (HIVE WORLD)

GHREDDASK (GARRISON WORLD)

BORAS MINOR (MINING WORLD)

THE TEARS OF THE EMPEROR

SABLE

ULTIMA SEGMENTUM

FORMUND

SOMNIUM STARS

KAR DUNIASH

CORINTHE

ATTILA

Temporary Rift Corridor

CIRILLO PRIME

THE YMGA MONOLITH

SCHINDELGHEIST

T'AU EMPIRE

NECRON SAUTEKH DYNASTY

HADEX ANOMALY

CHARADON SECTOR

ICHAR IV

THE SCOURGE STARS

MACRAGGE

PERDUS

BLACK REACH

NECRON NIHILAKH DYNASTY

FALSE HOPE

SALEM

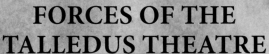

FORCES OF THE TALLEDUS THEATRE

The battle for the Talledus System was shaped by three major engagements: the bitter struggle for Benediction, the engine war upon Ghreddask, and the shadow hunt that played out amidst the Tears of the Emperor.

IMPERIUM

DEFENDERS OF THE GRAND HONORIFICUM

Order of Our Martyred Lady	3 Preceptories
Ghreddask Armoured	13 regiments
Ghreddask Artillery	9 regiments
Ghreddask Infantry	26 regiments
Cadian Auxilia	14 regiments
Sentae Honorifica	50,000 souls [est.]
Pilgrims of the River	[unknown numbers]
Trevortian Gladii	177 scratch companies
Censerhosts	36 formations

TALLEDUS RELIEF GROUP – BATTLEFLEET PHARAS

Salamanders	1 Demi-company
Black Templars	Gladius strike force
White Scars	3 Vanguard strike forces
Cadian 17th Infantry	(Regulators)
Cadian 567th Armoured	(Steelhounds)
Cadian 991st Armoured	(The Bloody 991st)

++ DATA PRESENTED AS RECOVERED ON 113.155//14. INCOMPLETE AND SUBJECT TO ALTERATION.

Additional forces dispatched to Talledus System according to Priority Order Sygna//X32.

CHAOS

BENEDICTION INVASION FORCE

Word Bearers	1 company
Brotherhood of the Knife	[unknown numbers]
Cult of Loss	[unknown numbers]
Bloodhounds	13 war parties
Gore Legion of Khoros	1 host

SIEGE OF GHREDDASK

Iron Warriors	1 company
House Khomentis	household strength
House Vrachul	household strength
Rusthammer Traitor Artillery	3 regiments
Vrachul Dragoons	2 regiments
Wyreblood Combat-Servitors	45 packs

CHAOS RAIDERS

Night Lords	3 warbands [approx.]
Siren Fleet	[unknown numbers]
Sons of Vengeance	[sightings reported]

Full analysis of Heretic forces unavailable due to extreme empyric disruption. Above record has been gathered from intercepted vox transmissions and astropathic messages.

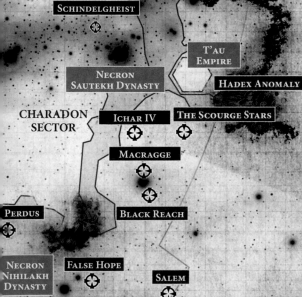

SEEDS OF CORRUPTION

The ruling priesthood of the Veritus Sub-sector may have believed that their domain was an incorruptible bastion of the Imperial Creed, but in truth the seeds of heresy had lurked unnoticed within its borders for many years.

It was the infamous Kor Phaeron, Keeper of the Faith and confidant of the Daemon Primarch Lorgar, who plotted the ruin of the Talledus System. None bore more hatred and contempt for the mortal servants of the God-Emperor than Phaeron, who had played a pivotal role in the earth-shattering events of the Horus Heresy. Veritus was the symbol of everything he despised: ignorance, weakness and petty mortal greed. Moreover, he believed that if the great shrine world of Benediction were to fall, it would spread pure terror across Segmentum Solar, a fear that could be exploited and harnessed to further empower the Dark Gods. One world would fall, then another and another.

Even before the nightmare of the Great Rift, heretic cults had emerged across the Talledus, Leonus and Keyfire Systems, seeded by the Dark Apostles of the Word Bearers. These prophets and demagogues did not yet encourage open worship of Chaos, for they knew that such overt displays of heresy would draw the full ire of the Ecclesiarchy and the Holy Ordos down upon them.

Instead, they cultivated certain sub-cults and splinter sects of Imperial faith that had been barely tolerated, or in some cases actively persecuted, by the Adeptus Ministorum, such as the Witnessers of Boras Minor, who believed that only by enduring appalling grief and loss could one become close to the God-Emperor. Other targeted cults included the ascetics of the Pherene Brotherhood, who saw divinity in humbleness and vows of silence, and the Cult of the Cleansing Comet, who dwelt within the deadly asteroid field on the edge of the Talledus known as the Tears of the Emperor, seeking to commune with their sacred deity.

All of these sects had suffered greatly at the hands of Cardinal Morst Bolifax, regent of the Veritus Sub-sector and a staunch traditionalist. Suspicious of the deviations of faith that had developed in his domain, Bolifax initiated a series of purges to remove subversive figures who dared to deviate from the unequivocal truth of the Imperial Creed. He sent his most fervent missionaries forth to cleanse these impurities. Shrines and shantytowns were burned, tomes and scriptures seized, and more than ten thousand apostates were crucified or stoned to death for their heathen practices. A dozen sub-cults of the Imperial Creed were condemned as heretical by the cardinal's decree. Anyone found practising their beliefs or rituals was to be subject to immediate torture and execution.

What remained of these sects were infiltrated by charismatic orators and zealous iconoclasts in thrall to the Dark Gods, and directed by the masters of the Word Bearers. At first these figureheads preached the supremacy of the God-Emperor. They railed against the tyrannical rule of the Ministorum Priests and the purges and executions they had inflicted upon innocent souls, for a simple divergence of belief. Stirring up anger and a simmering resentment against the cruel Bolifax, they compared his excesses to those of the infamous Goge Vandire.

The brutality of Bolifax's crackdown was the perfect gift for the cultist demagogues of Veritus. By playing upon the climate of fear and hatred, it was almost too easy for them to indoctrinate new followers in the worship of the Chaos Pantheon, and an ever-growing number of disenchanted pilgrims were driven into their clutches. Patiently, they sowed the seeds of true heresy, hiding the nature of their foul beliefs behind metaphor and rhetoric. Soul by soul they cultivated flocks of the damned and established cells upon distant worlds, even the gleaming capital

> *'Talledus is a grand deception, a symbol of the weakness and ignorance that taints the blood of the Imperium. I will visit upon it the truth of the Dark Pantheon.'*
>
> *- Kor Phaeron, Keeper of the Faith*

of Benediction itself. The Dark Apostles of the Word Bearers continued to direct this shadow war from afar, all the while preparing for their eventual assault upon Talledus.

Calling upon thousand-year-old debts and oaths, Kor Phaeron, the Dark Cardinal, assembled a conglomeration of allies from across several Traitor Legions and Renegade Chapters. The piratical Night Lords warmonger Yharas Kine was swayed with

promises of pious souls to torment and the finest pickings of a resource-rich system. The Iron Warriors assented to join the destruction, though they had little interest in the great war of faith espoused by Kor Phaeron, and sought only a testing ground for their daemonic war-engines. The Infernal houses of Vrachul and Khomentis pledged their Chaos Knights to the unholy cause, and millions of cultists and traitorous guard regiments were readied, ritually scarred, and branded with sigils of conviction.

The grand work gathered pace as the galaxy grew darker. Ruinous hexagrammatic patterns were laid down, monuments of fell power erected, and mass sacrifices prepared. Industrial cults upon the mining world of Coras Veltis used immense excavation lasers to burn eight-pointed stars into the bedrock of the planet. The Witnessers of Boras Minor, now calling themselves the Cult of Loss, slipped into the spacelanes of Satropol, infiltrating its tightly packed docking arms and smuggling in weapons and improvised explosives as they awaited the moment of their uprising. Chaos cults grew in strength, their numbers swelling daily.

And then, with a birth scream that dragged untold billions of malformed horrors into reality, the Great Rift broke open across the galaxy. Proud Cadia fell, the last barrier between the Eye of Terror and the Segmentum Solar. Daemonic entities manifested upon Holy Terra, and the Blood God Khorne closed his fist around the heart of Humanity. To Kor Phaeron's fury, there were whispers that Primarch Roboute Guilliman had returned, he who had once driven a power claw into the heart of the Dark Cardinal. Only after receiving a warp-granted vision of the resurrected Primarch departing from Terra, at the head of an enormous crusade, did Kor Phaeron unleash the hounds of war.

No less than thirteen massive battleships carved into the Talledus System, each blood red and daubed with the iconography of the corrupted XVII Legion. Eight of these planet-killing behemoths made a course for Benediction, while the remainder set out for the system's other prominent worlds. Accompanying this invasion force was an armada of lesser vessels, night-black reaver ships, rusted hulks and cargo cutters. As the Word Bearers' invasion fleet smashed into the outnumbered and outgunned Battlefleet Sentanis, responsible for the defence of Benediction, it also vomited forth a hail of razor-spiked Dreadclaw Drop Pods. The inhabitants of the glorious shrine world looked to the skies and saw a rain of fire. As the Word Bearers commenced their assault, the cults they had so patiently seeded across the system rose up in armed rebellion, and the astropathic relays of Boras Minor and Ghreddask fell silent. Talledus was alone, and the enemy was at its threshold.

DARKNESS DESCENDS

As the hordes of Chaos descended upon the Talledus System, all hope seemed lost. Yet, even as flames engulfed the shrine capital of Benediction and daemonic monstrosities spilled across the surface of multiple worlds, the faith of the God-Emperor's flock manifested in new and terrifying ways.

ONSLAUGHT OF CHAOS

Kor Phaeron knew that the success of the Chaos invasion of Talledus relied upon laying claim to its capital of Benediction. The Dark Cardinal was obsessed with symbology and ritual, and knew that this shining embodiment of the Imperial Creed must burn. Only when the highest spires of the Grand Honorificum were scrawled with the symbols of the Dark Gods and littered with the impaled bodies of the Corpse Emperor's servants would the will of Talledus' subjects truly be broken. His own Word Bearers spearheaded the assault on this vital target, slaughtering its defenders and any mortals foolish enough to deny the primacy of the Pantheon. Yet the Dark Cardinal of the Word Bearers was well aware that if the Imperials could isolate the battle at Benediction, then they could bring fearsome numbers to bear against the Chaos invasion force. This was where Phaeron's tentative allies would prove their worth.

Even before the Word Bearers had fired their first shots upon the surface of Benediction, Yharas Kine and his Night Lords warband had drawn the first blood of the Talledus conflict. A kill team of Night Lords specialists had descended upon the astropathic relay at Satrapol, butchering its occupants before setting off a cyclonic charge at the heart of the complex. At the same time, the battleship *Nightmare of Celyx* slipped from the warp at the far edge of the Talledus System. This cursed vessel contained thousands upon thousands of captured Astropaths, strapped into engines of torment and watched over by sinister warriors of the Night Lords.

The sons of Curze had performed the most horrific tortures upon these luckless souls, driving them into a state of constant pain-addled frenzy. Their combined psychic scream echoed out across the stars, interfering with long-range vox communications and scrambling the minds of ship-borne Navigators. Imperial reinforcements were dragged out of the warp into the killing fields of the Tears of the Emperor, the blazing asteroid-field at the rimward edge of the Talledus System. There, the Night Lords' fleet waited, anticipating a feast of terror and plunder.

Meanwhile the Iron Warriors, under the command of Warpsmith Etrogar, were tasked with containing the forces at Ghreddask, the system's formidably defended bastion world. The Warpsmith saw the outer planets of the Talledus System as the perfect testing ground for newly perfected monstrosities – the soul harvesters. These horrific creations were spaceborne fortress-factories that consisted of a central Daemonforge, surrounded by snaking tentacles of hellforged metal. These parasitic engines would embed themselves deep into a planet's crust, their boarding tentacles disgorging Iron Warriors into weak points in their enemy's defences. Meanwhile, the roaring furnace at the structure's heart would feed upon flesh, metal and the souls of the slain in order to spew out fresh Daemon Engine reinforcements.

As far as Kor Phaeron was concerned, these assaults were merely a diversion for his grand assault upon Benediction. They would divide Imperial reinforcements, securing him the time he needed to oversee the destruction of Benediction and its rebirth as a shrine of worship to the Chaos Pantheon.

THE IMPERIUM MOBILISES

The assault upon Talledus came entirely without warning, and the system's significant Astra Militarum presence was left reeling before the Chaos onslaught. On the surface of Benediction, a makeshift coalition of shattered Imperial Guard regiments fell back to the Grand Honorificum, there uniting under the command of Canoness Serita of the Order of Our Martyred Lady.

Battlefleets Ios and Cemeres – orbiting the bastion world of Ghreddask prior to the assault – suffered terrible losses as they attempted short-range warp jumps to the embattled capital. Warp interference claimed the lives of dozens of Navigators, their skulls bursting in a shower of bone and gore, unable to contain the magnitude of the Night Lords' corrupted signal. Others felt themselves inexorably drawn towards the psychic scream of desperation.

On all fronts the Chaos forces surged forward, their momentum

terrifying to behold. Upon the surface of Benediction itself, the Word Bearers – under the direction of Kor Phaeron – committed terrible atrocities and mass executions, weakening the fragile membrane between reality and the warp.

Within the Sanctum Solaris, at the heart of the Grand Honorificum, more than ten thousand priests, acolytes and non-militant Sororitas gathered in communal prayer, not moving, eating or taking water for days, even as the guns of the Word Bearers thundered relentlessly. They prayed to the God-Emperor for salvation and the light of their faith was a furious beacon, visible from far across the cold blackness of space.

Just as the hour seemed darkest, the Honorificum's long-range prognosticator arrays picked up a surge of activity on the coreward edge of the Talledus System. At first it was feared that this new presence was merely another fleet of Chaos warships, but a macro-encoded vox transmission from the strike cruiser *Fulminating Hammer* brought the first signs of hope to the beleaguered defenders of Benediction; Captain Mir'san of the Salamanders had heard the pleas of the faithful, and led a spearhead of Adeptus Astartes warriors to the defence of Talledus.

At his ritual site on the banks of the River Carmine, within an eight-pointed star made up of the bloodied corpses of saints and warriors, Kor Phaeron saw the arrival of the Imperial warfleet. Such a response had been expected, of course, and the appropriate preparations had been made. As far as Phaeron was concerned, it was all the better that the Corpse Emperor's lapdogs were here to witness the brutal fall of Benediction.

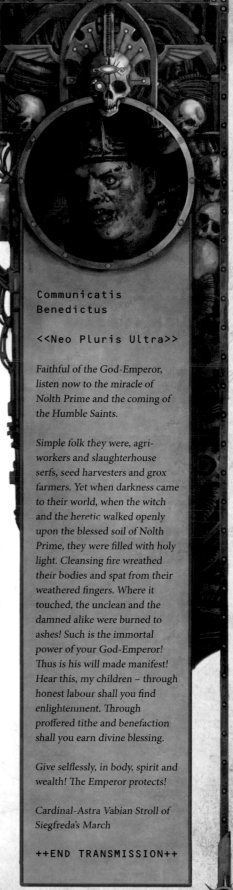

Communicatis
Benedictus

<<Neo Pluris Ultra>>

Faithful of the God-Emperor, listen now to the miracle of Nolth Prime and the coming of the Humble Saints.

Simple folk they were, agri-workers and slaughterhouse serfs, seed harvesters and grox farmers. Yet when darkness came to their world, when the witch and the heretic walked openly upon the blessed soil of Nolth Prime, they were filled with holy light. Cleansing fire wreathed their bodies and spat from their weathered fingers. Where it touched, the unclean and the damned alike were burned to ashes! Such is the immortal power of your God-Emperor! Thus is his will made manifest! Hear this, my children – through honest labour shall you find enlightenment. Through proffered tithe and benefaction shall you earn divine blessing.

Give selflessly, in body, spirit and wealth! The Emperor protects!

Cardinal-Astra Vabian Stroll of Siegfreda's March

++END TRANSMISSION++

FLAMES OF HERESY

The Word Bearers converged upon the capital world of Benediction with the full fury of their blasphemous hosts, unleashing hordes of ravening Daemons and frenzied cultists upon the unprepared shrine world. Yet Benediction was not without formidable champions of its own.

DARK ONSLAUGHT

The fury of the Word Bearers' assault brought terror to the surface of Benediction. Dreadclaws punched through the stained armaglass ceilings of mausoleums and devotional halls, and access hatches slammed down to reveal warriors in blood-red power armour. Scraps of parchment scrawled with profane runes dangled from their battle plates and their eyes blazed with conviction. These killers marched beneath the banners of the Dark Gods, bellowing catechisms of hate as their bolters unleashed a hail of devastation upon the world's overwhelmed Imperial Guard garrison. The Ghreddask 37th Armoured and 101st Infantry regiments – whose impressive battle record had granted them the honour of maintaining a permanent guard over the Honorificum – were taken entirely by surprise at the speed and brutality of the assault.

Worse still, hidden Chaos cults emerged to throw themselves upon the defenders, spilling from the planet's underwarrens in their millions to join their masters in sacred battle. In little more than half a day, the grounds surrounding the Honorificum were in Chaos hands. Amidst the shattered skeletons of cathedrums and shrines, rituals of mass sacrifice and slaughter were being performed on an industrial scale as the Word Bearers sought to draw forth daemonic reinforcements. Kor Phaeron himself oversaw these occult ceremonies, even as batteries of corrupted artillery hurled a ceaseless barrage of warp-laden shells into the psy-tech force field that surrounded the Honorificum.

Captain Mir'san's demi-company of Salamanders was greatly outnumbered by the Word Bearers host. The sons of Vulkan nonetheless went about their craft with stoic efficiency, clearing a beachhead amidst the mausoleum complexes of the Honorificum's outer grounds with flame-spewing Aggressors and Centurion Devastators. Captain Mir'san desired to dictate and confine the flow of battle by harrying the main concentration of the enemy, attempting to draw them into diverting their strength to engage the Salamanders. In this way further civilian casualties could be lessened, and the Space Marines could bear the brunt of the

BENEDICTION

A monument to the Ecclesiarchy's limitless funds and penchant for unrestrained grandeur, Benediction is the capital world of the Veritus Sub-sector and one of the most influential planets in the Segmentum Solar. Temple-cities and labyrinthine devotional trails cover nine-tenths of its surface, and the only areas not built upon consist of immense artificial waterways clogged by the floating shanty-fleets of hopeful pilgrims and itinerant missionaries. A smog of censer-smoke hangs like a shroud over the shrine world, infusing everything with the pungent scent of sacred oils and herbs.

Largest of all the planet's structures is the Grand Honorificum, a star-scraping cathedrum that houses the chambers of Cardinal Bolifax and a fortress-sanctuary of the Order of Our Martyred Lady. A psy-tech forcefield of Vigilant construction envelops the Honorificum, impenetrable to all but the most ferocious, planet-killing weaponry. Its soaring arch-spires are home to seven enormous macro-flak batteries littered with heavy guns and organ-rocket arrays. The Honorificum is the centre of Ecclesiarchal power in the Veritus Sub-sector, the repository in which the system's masses of gold tithes and indulgences are gathered. This domed superstructure stands upon an immense, man-made island, surrounded by the blessed waters of the River Carmine. Four great bridges span this waterway, lined with statues of past Ecclesiarchs and legendary heroes of the Imperial Creed.

The most recent planetary census estimated the population of Benediction to be somewhere in the region of one hundred billion souls, though the transitory nature of its populace, and the constant flow of wayfaring devotees from neighbouring systems, make that number impossible to verify.

assault. However, attempts to reinforce the eastern flank of the loyalist defenders were driven back by kill-packs of Possessed warriors and a fresh surge of cultist forces. Kor Phaeron would not take Captain Mir'san's proffered bait; the Grand Honorificum remained his focus, for with its fall the Dark Cardinal would deal a mortal blow to the Imperial faith.

Although they were sorely pressed, the warriors of the Order of Our Martyred Lady defended the four great bridges leading to the heart of the Honorificum with stubborn resolve. Warriors clad in obsidian power armour sang hymnals to the saints of Benediction and to their beloved God-Emperor as they fired back against the blasphemous horde. Exorcist tanks sang, unleashing spiralling volleys of sacred rockets that pulverised entire formations of heretic invaders. The roar of heavy flamers and the thunderous bark of Godwyn-D'eaz-pattern bolters formed a deafening percussion to accompany the psalms of the faithful.

It was a brave and spirited defence, but it could not last. The blood of thousands of flayed priests spilled into the crystal waters of the River Carmine as Kor Phaeron's rituals came to a gruesome crescendo. As the river turned crimson, it began to bubble and boil with motion. Hideous shapes crawled from the corrupted waters, wielding brazen blades and howling in savage delight. The River Carmine itself broke its banks and surged forward towards the psy-shield of the Grand Honorificum. A tidal wave of superheated gore swallowed hundreds of Battle Sisters and guardsmen, and turned battle tanks and artillery emplacements alike into iron slurry. The moment it struck the shimmering shield of the Honorificum, the defences of the great cathedrum fizzled and died. The way to the heart of Benediction was open and Kor Phaeron led his warriors forth with bellowing

praises to the Dark Gods, they themselves taken aback by the potency of their warpcraft. Breaches in reality torn open by ritual and incantation continued to grow, drawing forth not just hordes of minor entities, but the leathery, bat-winged shapes of Greater Daemons. Bolts of summoned warp energy erupted into coruscating fireballs, and in the heat of battle several Word Bearers fell, convulsing as hungering mouths and other strange mutations burst through skin and ceramite. Entire districts of Benediction were overrun, and Daemons spilled into the halls of the Grand Honorificum itself, where the Sisters of Battle staged a desperate, room-by-room stand.

MIRACLE OF THE SAINT'S WALL

With the collapse of the last bastion between the Word Bearers and the heart of Benediction, the battle for the capital world seemed decided. Yet Canoness Serita and her warriors refused to give in to despair. They fought with selfless dedication and fury, striking out with gun butts, blades and chainswords when ammunition ran dry. Those who looked upon this valorous stand were filled with a holy fire. Civilians and cosseted ministers alike took up weapons against the forces of Chaos. At first, the Word Bearers and their daemonic allies laughed at such

pitiful defiance. Yet, as the blood of the faithful spilled, spears of golden light broke through the stained armaglass windows of the Honorificum. As the prayers of the God-Emperor's servants echoed over screams and gunfire it seemed, to astonished onlookers, that the dead souls of Benediction arose to protect the living.

Golden, skull-faced spirits swept forth from ancient tombs and reliquaries, rising high into the heavens to encircle the Grand Honorificum. These manifestations formed a shield of impassable light, a radiant halo that filled the faithful who looked upon it with renewed hope. Daemons and heretics that attempted to force their way through this aegis of faith were burned to ashes. Even the Word Bearers' artillery could not force a breach in the shield. Where the golden light of the Saint's Wall shone, the barrier between reality and the nightmare realm of the warp was remade.

Kor Phaeron could only look on in fury as great swathes of the daemonic army he had summoned disintegrated into nothingness, howling in impotent rage as their connection to the material realm was severed. Inspired by the bizarre phenomenon they had witnessed, Mir'san's Salamanders launched fresh assaults on the advance formations of the Word Bearers, breaking through to the bridge over the River Carmine and cutting the heretic force in two.

The battle for Benediction had not been decided by any measure, but the momentum of the Word Bearers' assault had been repelled, and the Grand Honorificum remained in loyalist hands. Still, the Dark Cardinal had no intention of retreating, not with Benediction so nearly in his grasp. Whispers filtered out across the tides of the warp, dark communiques summoning Chaos reinforcements to the Talledus theatre.

WRATH OF IRON

Even as the fighting for Benediction escalated to new heights of savagery, the Iron Warriors drew Imperial reinforcements into a brutal war of attrition on the world of Ghreddask.

DAEMONIC INDUSTRY

Warpsmith Etrogar had no interest in Kor Phaeron's grand plans for the Talledus System. A ruthlessly practical soul, Etrogar saw the rampant psychic disturbance unleashed by the Great Rift not as a spiritual awakening, but as an infinite source of power to be harnessed. The Warpsmith entered Talledus at the helm of the soul harvester *Scarax Krond*. More spaceborne factory than starship, this cephalopodic metal monster was powered by an immense Daemonforge. A product of the Iron Warriors' darkest experiments in metallomorphosis and warp-engineering, it would be the first such creation to be tested in battle.

With its vast alpine ranges and city-sized citadel fortresses, the bastion world of Ghreddask was the most heavily defended planet in the Talledus System, aside from Benediction itself. Its seven great hive cities provided billions of souls for the Astra Militarum, and its deep reserves of promethium and super-dense minerals only added to Ghreddask's critical value to the Imperium – making it an irresistible target for Etrogar.

The *Scarax Krond* latched onto the surface of Ghreddask like an immense parasite, thrusting pseudopods the size of hab-blocks deep into the earth. These snaking tentacles pulverised their way through rock and stone with siege drills and melta-cannons, before bursting up from the earth within the walls of Ghreddask's citadel fortifications. Heretic

Astartes warriors marched forth, unleashing deadly volleys of bolt rounds into their unprepared foes. At the same time, Chaos Knights of House Khomentis lumbered from the gatehouse of *Scarax Krond*, bellowing oaths of destruction as they set upon the armoured formations of the Astra Militarum.

Tank after tank was blasted into molten slag, and arcs of heavy bolter fire obliterated entire formations of Ghreddask infantry. All the while the Daemonforge of the *Scarax Krond* glutted itself upon the aura of death and destruction. Blasted corpses and twisted wreckages of shattered war machines were shovelled into its furnaces, as Etrogar and his fellow Warpsmiths stoked the hellish fires with the souls of the slain. The *Scarax Krond* spewed out a tide of Daemon Engines, from scuttling, spider-like Venomcrawlers to hulking Maulerfiends that galloped into battle, eager to mutilate and destroy. Soon the loyalists were in full flight, retreating to the polar citadel of Fortress Resolve, where they prepared to make their final stand.

FORLORN HOPE

Just as the cruisers of the Iron Warriors prepared orbital bombardments that would blast open the last vestiges of resistance on Ghreddask, the Chaos fleet picked up a surge of warp disturbance. Two enemy capital ships dropped out of orbit – black vessels, bearing the stark white cross of the righteous Black Templars Chapter.

Castellan Dramos led a single strike force detached from the Rutherian

Addendum 06:6/A

<<Vox Transmission Received — Priority Viridian Maxis>>

This is Interrogator Harkin, broadcasting [unintelligible] safe house Prima Gladian. This is a distress call, Priority Viridian Maxis, on frequency oh-seven-eight, alpha-nexus-carmine. Oh, Holy Throne! [exchange of gunfire, unidentified sound signature]

[unintelligible] breached the cordon. Yhascon and the others are dead, or worse. It's just me. It's just me. I don't have long. [unintelligible] was never a weapon, like we thought. It was a gate, and +++ REDACTED +++ The Oddreon System is dead. Do not come here. That's what they want. They want you to come for us, but by the God-Emperor you have to stay away.

[static burst, possible detonation]

The Emperor protects! The Emperor protects! The–[gunfire, followed by protracted screaming]

++END TRANSMISSION++

Crusade, all that could be spared due to the Templars' extensive campaigns elsewhere across the Segmentum Solar. Fortunately, Dramos could also call upon a cadre of Imperial Knights from House Mortan, commanded by the dour yet ferocious Sir Dirkwald. Dramos scanned the latest tactical cogitations broadcast from Fortress Resolve. The situation was grim. The Iron Warriors were besieging the polar citadel, pouring daemonic forces against its shield-walls while their siege tanks kept up a relentless bombardment. Yet the true threat, Dramos quickly intuited, was the *Scarax Krond*. As long as the Daemonforge was operational, the traitors could replenish their forces indefinitely. Strike Force Dawnhammer would deploy in a decisive attack upon the soul harvester.

The warriors of House Mortan made for the surface of Ghreddask in their fortified bulwark-landers, the heavily armoured vessels shrugging off reams of flak fire. Sir Dirkwald led a frontal assault upon the *Scarax Krond*. From the parapets of the soul harvester, Iron Warriors poured a stream of fire down upon the advancing loyalists. While the Knights drew the attention of the Chaos defenders, squads of Inceptors descended upon the soul harvester like living comets, burning through the upper atmosphere and locking co-ordinates upon the pulsing shell of the *Scarax Krond*. They struck home with shattering force, breaching holes in the fleshmetal carapace with demolition charges, even as they fended off flocks of fire-spitting Heldrakes. Castellan Dramos led the assault into the heart of the *Scarax Krond*, battling through the innards of the iron monster, alongside a retinue of veteran Crusaders.

This assault team suffered grievous losses as the Iron Warriors assailed them at every turn, but in an act of self-sacrifice that would mark their names in the honour-scrolls of their order, Dramos and his command squad managed to detonate a cyclonic charge at the heart of the structure.

The resulting warp explosion swept through the soul harvester, immolating loyalist and heretic alike and blasting its assembly halls and charnel-factories to atoms. The *Scarax Krond* convulsed and thrashed its metal tendrils like a wounded animal, but its daemonic furnaces would not be snuffed out so easily. Dramos' sacrifice had bought the defenders of Ghreddask precious time, but the planet's fate still hung in the balance.

ANCIENT OATHS

The conflict that raged upon Ghreddask was dominated by the presence of super-heavy war machines and enormous armoured battalions. Striding through the hailstorm of shells and rocket barrages came the towering forms of Imperial Knights, as well as their dark mirror, the dreaded Chaos Knights. Both of these bitter enemies upheld ancient oaths to their liege lords with unwavering certainty. In the case of the corrupted houses, their refusal to break bonds of honour had found them fighting on the wrong side of the Horus Heresy, supporting the traitorous forces of Warmaster Horus as they made war upon the Imperium of Mankind.

House Mortan provided the majority of the loyalist war engines on Ghreddask, with no less than six Knights hailing from the darksome world of Kimdaria. Veteran beast-hunters all, the Mortan Knights hailed from a world wreathed in perpetual darkness and ravaged by predatory behemoths, a harsh place that had forged iron-hard souls. They proved invaluable in the battle against the Daemon Engines of the *Scarax Krond*, corralling the twisted abominations with fleet Armigers before tearing them apart with reaper chainswords and thunderstrike gauntlets.

Warpsmith Etrogar had forged pacts with Houses Khomentis and Vrachul, both of whom were sworn to serve the Dark Mechanicum – the unholy counterpart to the Adeptus Mechanicus. The war machines of Vrachul belched acidic vapours from vents and exhaust ports; a pall of chemical smog wreathed them in battle, dissolving the flesh and armour of anything that strayed within its bounds. The warriors of Khomentis kept daemonic spirits as hunting thralls and took cruel delight in chasing down and brutalising wounded and damaged Imperial Knights. Both Houses favoured the rush and crash of close combat, a craving that the loyalist nobles of House Mortan were only too glad to accommodate. Ghreddask shook to the impact of titan-killing weaponry as these two ancient foes duelled, prepared to fight to the bitter end.

SCREAMS IN THE VOID

Yharas Kine and his Night Lords warband found rich pickings amidst the asteroid field known as the Tears of the Emperor. Broadcasting a terrible psychic signal, they lured their prey into darkness before hunting and tormenting them with sadistic delight. Their latest quarry, however, would not prove such an easy kill.

TEARS OF AGONY

The *Nightmare of Celyx* drifted through the Tears of the Emperor, broadcasting its terrible signal across the stars. Following the siren ship closely were the shadowed hulls of Night Lords vessels. As Imperial cruisers and escort ships were dragged off course into the belt, these reaver ships would strike hard and fast, firing boarding hooks and unleashing hunting parties of Heretic Astartes upon their stricken prey. Such was the horror let loose by the Night Lords that the Tears of the Emperor burned blood red. The asteroid field was visible from the surface of Talledus' war-torn worlds, a ragged wound in the sky that promised a bloody and terrible end.

As the battle for the Talledus System raged on, more and more desperately needed reinforcements disappeared. Driven mad by the strength of the psychic broadcast, Navigators were drawn unerringly into the Night Lords' trap. Astra Militarum generals and officers

of the fleet despaired, for every lost ship was a heavy blow to the Imperium's hopes of containing the Talledus conflict.

Salvation came from an unexpected quarter. A strike force of Vanguard Space Marines from the White Scars Chapter, under the command of Jodagha Khan, had been tracking the movements of Yharas Kine's Night Lords for several months, following the psychic spoor of the Heretic Astartes' tortured victims. The White Scars had witnessed first-hand the trail of horror that the Heretic Astartes had left in their wake, and their revulsion at the depravity of their fallen brethren was absolute. The Khan's stealth cruisers followed the flight of the *Nightmare of Celyx* straight to Talledus, and to the Tears of the Emperor.

There the Khan and his battle-brothers found a graveyard of torn and twisted vessels, orbited by flayed, vacuum-frozen corpses still wearing expressions of agony. There

was no sign of the siren ship itself, but the sudden shriek of proximity sensors revealed a host of incoming vessels – dagger-shaped Night Lords strike craft raging toward them at full speed.

The resulting void battle was swift and brutal. The smaller Night Lords force had approached under the cover of drifting asteroids, and was upon the White Scars before the Space Marines could bring their lance batteries to bear. The cruiser *Thunderstone* was boarded by several kill-packs of Raptors, who wreaked terrible carnage upon the crew and sabotaged several motive systems before being driven off by squads of White Scars Infiltrators. As soon as the tide of battle turned, the Night Lords vessels slipped back into the impervious cover of the asteroid field.

DEATH HUNT

The Night Lords had turned the Tears of the Emperor into their hellish playground, mastering the

RISE OF TERROR

The Night Lords welcomed the coming of the Great Rift with relish. Fully half of the Imperium was wreathed in impenetrable darkness while the other half was left in confusion and chaos, leaving the piratical heretics to indulge their every depraved whim. Indeed, the remnant of the 8th Legion, who had been reduced to an existence of piracy and reaving in order to replenish their battle gear and numbers, prospered like never before.

Munitorum worlds were stripped bare by night-clad warriors. Several Space Marine fortress-monasteries were raided, gene-seed stolen and armouries emptied, defenders mutilated and ritually

slaughtered. Worse still, the legion's Chaos Sorcerers devised new methods of exploiting Humanity's weakened state. These methods were as cunning as they were unthinkably cruel; thousands of Astropaths were abducted and subjected to agonising torment, for the sons of Curze had learnt how to use the combined psychic trauma of their victims to create siren signals that would divert or lure stranded Imperial vessels into their clutches.

The Night Lords learned to practice this dark art on a grand scale. Entire worlds were transformed into monuments to pain and terror, and the sons of Curze delighted in every gruesome atrocity.

deadly, shifting battleground and turning it against their foes. The White Scars found themselves not only assailed by the Heretic Astartes, but staggered by the devious traps and lures that the Night Lords had assembled throughout the asteroid field – planetoids laced with cyclonic charges and astropathic signals that drew the White Scars into pre-prepared killing zones.

Only the multi-spectrum precognition arrays of the White Scars' stealth cruisers allowed them to navigate a path through the haunted darkness. So began a shadow war of escalating brutality, as the warriors of Chogoris sought to track down their hated foes through a maelstrom of blazing rocks and ruined spaceships. The Night Lords had spared the lives of the Navigators from these gutted vessels, though the survivors found themselves subject to a far worse fate than death. Flayed, agonised and kept alive and conscious by warp magic, they howled their torment into the void. These disruptive, psychic screams obscured the siren signal broadcast by the *Nightmare of Celyx*, rendering it all but impossible to discern the ship's exact location.

Each of these lures was an ambush site guarded by kill-packs of Night Lords Raptors, Chaos Space Marines and Daemon Engines. Whether they were located on drifting asteroids or the skeletons of dead vessels, every inch of ground was rigged with las-grid traps, scatter mines and booby-trapped corpses. Incursor Squads paid a heavy toll to clear out each ambush site, utilising their Divinator-class auspexes to fashion a full-spectrum analysis of the battlefield and disperse this vital combat data to their battle-brothers. Infiltrator Squads breached the lightless halls of dead ships, hurling smoke grenades and firing disciplined bursts from their augur-scoped marksman bolt carbines. The tenets of speed and constant movement, central to the art of warfare practised by the warriors of

Chogoris, were stymied by the Night Lords' devious tricks.

Yharas Kine and his contingent – masters of the art of stealth and subterfuge – delighted in the challenge provided by the Vanguard Space Marines. Claws of elite Chaos Terminators launched short-range teleportation strikes into the hearts of the White Scars formations, butchering and eviscerating with lightning claws and power axes. Heldrakes preyed upon the White Scars' dropships in the vacuum of space, and the nightmarish fiends known as Warp Talons breached the hulls of Space Marine cruisers, running amok in the darkness.

For all the cruel ingenuity of the Night Lords' attacks, the White Scars, under the command of the

Khan, adapted with remarkable speed. They feigned desperate retreats, drawing the traitor forces into kill zones of their own. Damaged ships were sacrificed to lure in those Night Lords drunk on the thrill of murder and torture. The ambushers suddenly became the ambushed as White Scars warriors appeared in their midst, yelling blood-curdling war cries and engaging the Heretic Astartes in brutal, close-quarter battles.

Yet even as the momentum of battle shifted from hour to hour, the *Nightmare of Celyx* remained unseen, still broadcasting its demented song. Until the White Scars had cut off every false signal, the desperate fighting within the Tears of the Emperor would continue.

Echoes of Awakening

The galaxy is caught in the grip of an empyric maelstrom caused by the birth of the Great Rift. The ripples from this disaster are felt across millions of worlds, giving rise to manifestations of psychic power both wondrous and horrifying. Reports gradually filter back to Terra, and Humanity begins to grasp the magnitude of events.

+++

```
Junior Commissar HR. Lei
Sub-tachia Offensive MISSID
OO:68TA — GZ West
```

```
Engaged forces of Dominaur Rhesk at
Hill 942. Enemy contingents numbered
approx. one thousand: significant
Hereticus Extremis presence. Losses
heavy, so Epsilon-class deployed.
```

```
Initial success. Reached Objective
Callus, but Epsilon-class displayed
increasing signs of potential
corruption. Commissar Koln initiated
prejudicial termination, but unable
to contain EXTREME warp incident.
Hill 942 destroyed. Repeat, entirely
destroyed. Battalion lost, HQ command
terminated. Requesting orders.
```

+++

```
Priority Missive //56D
Category: Xenos Aggressus
```

The Orks are gathering in vast numbers in the Glaaxian Corridor. Nothing stands between them and the sector capital. All contact lost with Battlefleets Rho and Pheilades. Significant and unprecedented warp disturbance across system. Nalmora and Port Gardia silent. The stars are green. All we can hear on the vox is the thunder of wardrums. Six hundred and eighty-six Astropaths have either dropped dead from cranial ruptures or were overcome by seizures and thereafter granted the Emperor's Mercy. By the stars of Sol, the drums are growing louder with every passing moment. I pray to the God-Emperor that this missive is received.

```
++ Communique received 14.74.613 Terran
sidereal. Demi-company of the Spears
of the Emperor diverted to investigate
Glaaxian Sub-sector. ++
```

+++

The galaxy will not perish in flames and fury. There will be no glorious final battle, no clash and crash of blades. I have dreamt of the death of Humanity, and we shall fall in silence.

+++

[Vox Intercept: Yhedaris System]

'Hear this, you simpering lapdogs! You servile, dull creatures. The Illuminator is coming! Yhedaris is but the first brushstroke upon a grand canvas. He is coming, and with him comes an endless carnival of sensation!'

Addendum: Vox transmission hails from the Cathedrum of the Ashen Heart on Ortus Prime. No response along priority channels. Multiple Heretic warships sighted traversing the Cascar Nebula, on a path towards Black Mantle. Iconography matches that of the Emperor's Children, Excommunicate Traitoris.

+++

Rejoice! The Sleeper awakens, and sings the song that ends the world! All across the stars His children stir, and rise to claim their mind's birthright. So it begins, and so it ends.

+++

Fall of the House of Tyr

Lord-Governor Tyr was assassinated in the early hours of 0.13.774 sidereal. Simultaneously, Rhynius Tyr and Lucea Ranolph-Tyr perished in an apparent explosion whilst taking part in the Micraxian Solar Regatta. The sole surviving members of Tyr's household staff speak of tall, long-limbed xenos armoured in black, who summoned gouts of witchfire to immolate the lord-governor. Forensic examinations of Tyr's property have uncovered stocks of illicit xenotech and heretical texts, as well as evidence of depraved rituals. The Micraxian Guard is mustering for a reprisal strike as of 0.14.13. I shall keep the Order informed as the situation evolves.

+++

+++

Prognosticatum Ultima: Prospero Exactis

Grand Master Voldus, the empyric imbalance along the Prosperan Rift is far worse than first feared. Daemonic incursions are reported on multiple vectors, and something far worse is brewing upon the surface of Sortiarius. A maelstrom builds there, a gathering of psychic power greater than anything we have witnessed since the opening of the Cicatrix Maledictum. Doubtless the Crimson King plans some new atrocity, though our Prognosticars could not pierce the arcane veil drawn about the Sorcerer's Planet. As scattered as our numbers are, I believe that we must investigate in force. I await your wisdom, Grand Master.

+++

Vox Echo:
Black Ship Fleet Thersius Last Recorded Location: Obrizar Nebulae

Reading catastrophic warp signatures across the fleet. Anti-empyric wardings failing on all vectors. Starscythe breached amidships, venting tithe-cargo into space. We have reports of gunfire in the restraint holds. No communication received from Sister Superior Dhaera since she led a pacification squad to Deck 600 at 00.646 hours. Captain Sentulla has enacted Extremis Doctrine Vermillion-Alpha. Have enacted critical power surge to warp engines. Detonation imminent. This is the last transmission of the Black Ship Tortantia. May the God-Emperor grant us mercy.

+++

Intercepted Dataslate 144/1525/CV — Marked for censure

It is a miracle, my friend. I have no other word for it. The fiends had broken through the Bastion Line and were upon us, tearing at our heels as we fled in panic. Yet, as we ran, I saw Sergeant Maklinnan hobbling towards thc swarm. His arm was missing and half his face was burned away by the xenos' acidic spew, but he had the most serene look in the remaining eye. He held up one hand and everything turned blindingly white. I heard the shrieks of alien filth and, when I opened my eyes, the ground was littered with smoking corpses. The few clawbeasts left alive recoiled and howled as if wreathed in invisible flames. As one the 145th turned and raised our bayonets to them.

+++

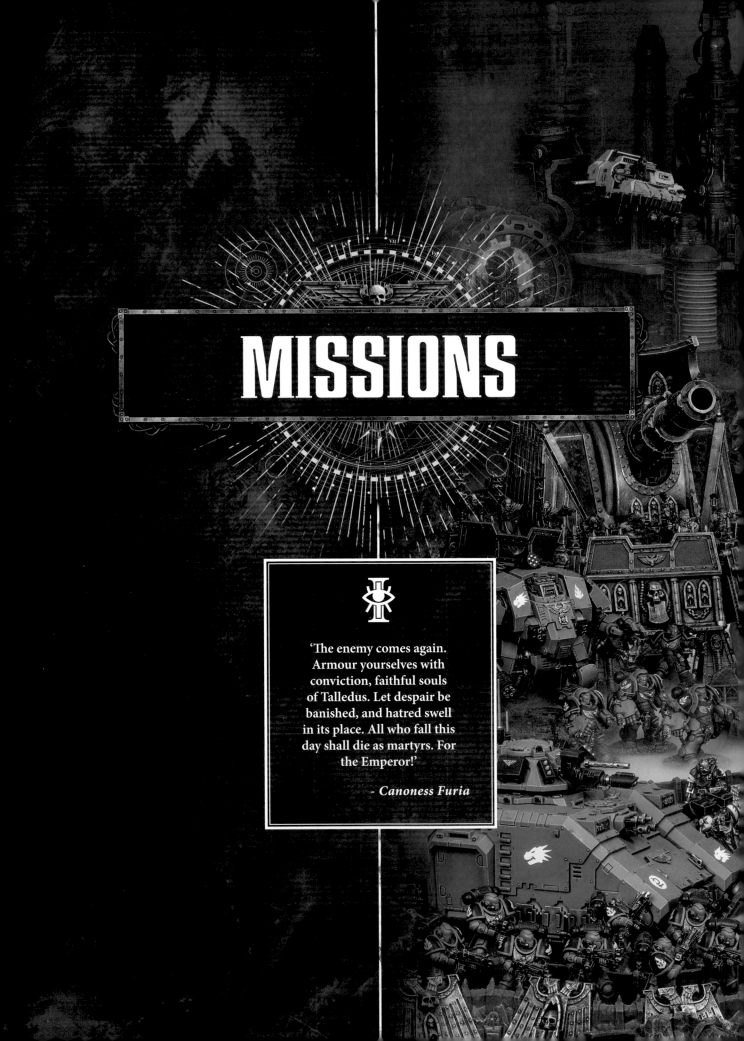

MISSIONS

'The enemy comes again.
Armour yourselves with
conviction, faithful souls
of Talledus. Let despair be
banished, and hatred swell
in its place. All who fall this
day shall die as martyrs. For
the Emperor!'

- *Canoness Furia*

UNHALLOWED GROUND

The rules presented in this section allow you to play games set in locations inspired by those found in the narrative of this book, as well as play through some of the most dramatic and climactic moments from the early stages of the Psychic Awakening, when the Chaos Legions began their assault upon the Talledus System.

THEATRES OF WAR

Opposite you will find rules for a new Theatre of War. Theatres of War allow you to play games of Warhammer 40,000 in evocative environments that present exciting and unique new challenges to overcome.

Theatre of War: Warp Tear is designed to represent any one of the numerous battlefields across which the fate of the people of Talledus was decided. Foul warp predations, made real through the unnatural influence of the Cicatrix Maledictum, brought forth innumerable horrors that preyed upon the loyal citizenry of the Imperium, who, with only their faith in the Emperor to protect them, clung to their beliefs as a form of strength in the face of such evils.

Although the Theatre of War opposite is designed to reflect the narrative of Faith and Fury, it can be used to represent any location where the fabric of reality, which separates the material realm from that of the empyrean, has become weak and fragile. In such places where malign psychic energies manifest themselves at will and the soul of every mortal hangs in the balance.

ECHOES OF WAR MISSIONS

On pages 26-29 you will find two new Echoes of War missions for your narrative battles. These allow you to refight key battles described in this book, from the surprise attack on the capital world of Benediction to the Iron Warriors' ground assault of the planet Ghreddask. These missions can be combined with the Theatre of War opposite to add an additional layer of depth to your games.

Players are also encouraged to use the rules that are presented here as a basis for their own narrative play missions, whether they are a part of the ongoing struggle for the Talledus System, or simply to represent other, similar battlefields upon which their armies wish to do battle.

THEATRES OF WAR

As the Psychic Awakening took hold of the Talledus System, fear and terror were met by faith and determination. The forces of the Imperium rose up in resistance as the heretical forces of the Dark Gods, alongside their daemonic allies, assailed them with firepower and the malefic energies of the warp.

In this section you will find an exciting new Theatre of War to use in your games of Warhammer 40,000. Theatres of War offer new tactical challenges to enrich your games, and introduce new rules to represent many varied battle environments. Some modify the core rules, for example, by altering the range of weapons. Some provide new rules for phenomena like dust storms, volcanic eruptions and earthquakes. Some grant additional abilities and Stratagems to certain units.

These rules are designed to reflect the increasingly erratic psychic phenomena that have manifested themselves in the Talledus System due to the growth of the Great Rift, but they are entirely optional and, so long as you and your opponent agree, can be used in any Warhammer 40,000 game.

Agree which, if any, Theatre of War rules will be used when you are setting up the battlefield, before deployment.

THEATRE OF WAR: WARP TEAR

As the Cicatrix Maledictum wrapped its tendrils around the Talledus System, the barrier that existed between reality and the anarchy of the warp grew weak and impermanent. Psychic powers, and the horrors that they brought, manifested themselves unabated as the rift continued to grow.

In the Dark Places: Before deployment, each player selects one piece of terrain on the battlefield to become a tear in reality. Whenever a unit starts or ends a move within 1" of any part of any of the selected terrain pieces, roll one D6; on a 4+ that unit suffers 1 mortal wound.

Faith and Desperation: When a Morale test is taken for a unit, on a roll of a 1, no models flee and that unit can make a move as if it were the controlling player's Movement phase.

Devoured by Warp Denizens: When the last model in a unit is destroyed, roll one D6 for each other unit that is within 3" of it before removing it from play. Subtract 1 from the result if the unit being rolled for is a CHARACTER. On a 4+ that unit suffers 1 mortal wound.

Boundless Energies: When a Psychic test is taken for a unit, after rolling the dice the controlling player can choose for that unit to harness the boundless energies of the warp; if they do, add 1 to the total. If the psychic power is successfully manifested and not resisted, that unit suffers 1 mortal wound after the psychic power is resolved.

ECHOES OF WAR
THE STAND AT SAINT'S WALL

The Salamanders' bold holding actions did little to divert Kor Phaeron's attention from his true prize. As his force of Word Bearers and depraved cultists crossed the bridges that marked the final approach to the Grand Honorificum, the Imperial defenders prepared to make their last stand.

THE ARMIES

Each player must first muster an army from their collection. The Defender commands the Imperial coalition that is tasked with the defence of the Grand Honorificum, consisting of Adepta Sororitas from the Order of Our Martyred Lady, the Salamanders Chapter of the Adeptus Astartes, and various Astra Militarum infantry regiments.

The Attacker commands the heretical forces of the Word Bearers.

A player can include any models in their army. If their army is Battle-forged, they will also be able to use the appropriate Stratagems included with this mission (see opposite).

THE BATTLEFIELD

The Defender creates the battlefield. The battlefield should be heavily fortified within the Defender's deployment zone to mark the perimeter of the Honorificum, while the rest of the battlefield is left sparse with roads representing the final approach to the shrine. At the centre of the Defender's battlefield edge, an objective marker should be placed onto a flat area of a terrain piece, to mark the entrance to the halls of the Honorificum that the Word Bearers are trying to breach.

DEPLOYMENT

After terrain has been set up, the Defender sets up their Adepta Sororitas and Astra Militarum units wholly within their deployment zone, while their Adeptus Astartes units are placed in Reserve (see page 194 of *Warhammer 40,000* rulebook). The Attacker then sets up their units wholly within their deployment zone.

PRELIMINARY BOMBARDMENT

Once both sides have been set up, the Attacker launches a Preliminary Bombardment (see page 194 of *Warhammer 40,000* rulebook).

FIRST TURN

The Attacker has the first turn.

HONORIFICUM PSY-SHIELD

In the first battle round, when resolving an attack made with a ranged weapon against a unit from the Defender's army, subtract 1 from the hit roll.

SUSTAINED ASSAULT

The Attacker can use the Sustained Assault rules (see the *Warhammer 40,000* rulebook). Units brought back to the battlefield using these rules must be set up wholly within 6" of the Attacker's battlefield edge.

ANGELS OF DEATH

Adeptus Astartes units arriving from Reserve must be set up wholly within 6" of either of the Defender Reinforcements' battlefield edges, and more than 6" away from any enemy models.

ENTER THE HALLS

At the end of any battle round, if the Attacker controls the objective marker, then the battle ends immediately (see Victory Conditions, below). A player controls an objective marker if they have more models within 3" of the centre of it than their opponent.

BATTLE LENGTH

Use the Random Battle Length rules (see page 194 of *Warhammer 40,000* rulebook) to determine how long the battle lasts.

VICTORY CONDITIONS

If, at the end of the battle, the Attacker controls the objective marker, the Attacker wins a major victory. Any other result is a major victory for the Defender.

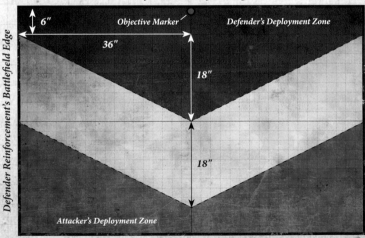

Defender's Battlefield Edge

6"

Objective Marker

Defender's Deployment Zone

36"

18"

Defender Reinforcement's Battlefield Edge

Defender Reinforcement's Battlefield Edge

18"

Attacker's Deployment Zone

Attacker's Battlefield Edge

STRATAGEMS

In this mission, the players can use Command Points (CPs) to use the following bonus Stratagems:

UNENDING HORDES
1CP

Attacker Stratagem

Under the auspices of the Great Rift, the Dark Cardinal's ceremonies unleashed untold numbers of Daemonkind upon the shrine's protectors.

Use this Stratagem at the start of the Morale phase. Select one **CHAOS DAEMON** unit from your army that contains a Daemonic Icon. Until the end of that phase, that unit's Daemonic Icon takes effect on a roll of 1-3, instead of 1.

SANCTUARY FOR THE PURE
1CP

Defender Stratagem

During the early stages of the battle, the Honorificum's powerful psy-shield kept the heretical assaults at bay.

Use this Stratagem at the start of the first battle round. Until the end of that battle round, whenever a model from the Defender's army would lose a wound as a result of a mortal wound, roll one D6; on a 6, that wound is not lost.

WAVE OF GORE
1CP

Attacker Stratagem

The River Carmine's waters surged their bunks, the ethereal flood burning away vast swathes from both sides.

Use this Stratagem at the start of your Movement phase. For each non-**DAEMON** unit on the battlefield, roll one D6; on a 5+ that unit suffers 1 mortal wound. You can only use this Stratagem once per battle.

RELIGIOUS FERVOUR
1CP

Defender Stratagem

Spurred on by the conviction of their fallen leaders, the Imperials swore vengeance upon their hated foes.

Use this Stratagem in any phase, when an **ADEPTA SORORITAS CHARACTER** from your army is destroyed. Until the end of the turn, when resolving an attack made with a melee weapon by a friendly unit within 3" of the destroyed model, re-roll a hit roll of 1 and re-roll a wound roll of 1.

CHAOTIC MUTATION
1CP

Attacker Stratagem

At the height of the battle for the Grand Honorificum, unbound energies took hold of many Word Bearers, granting them the dark blessing of mutation.

Use this Stratagem at the start of your Movement phase. Select one **WORD BEARERS INFANTRY** unit (**CHAOS CULTISTS** units cannot be chosen) to receive a mutation. Roll one D3 and look up the result below.

D3	Mutation
1	**Cloven Feet**: Add 2" to the Move characteristic of models in the unit.
2	**Unholy Vigour**: Each model in the unit adds 1 to its Strength and Toughness characteristics.
3	**Clawed Forelimbs**: Each model in the unit adds 1 to its Attacks characteristic.

The effects of this mutation last for the remainder of the battle. A unit can only be selected for this Stratagem once per battle.

GUARDIAN SOULS
1CP

Defender Stratagem

At the height of the slaughter, it appeared that the souls of the faithful rose to protect their comrades, returning to strike down the servants of the Dark Gods.

Use this Stratagem in your opponent's Shooting phase or the Fight phase, when the last model in a unit from your army is destroyed as a result of an attack made by a model in an enemy unit. Roll one D6; on a 2+ that enemy unit suffers D3 mortal wounds after it has finished making its attacks.

ECHOES OF WAR
UNDERGROUND INCURSION

When the Warpsmith Etrogar unleashed the fury of his daemonically infused engines upon Ghreddask, he launched the assault by using the *Scarax Krond* to tunnel a number of beachheads far behind enemy lines. This made it possible for his men to strike directly at the heart of the foe's command structure.

THE ARMIES

Each player must first muster an army from their collection. The Defender commands the Astra Militarum forces, manning a section of the hive city's defensive fortifications. As such, the Defender must take a Company Commander as their Warlord.

The Attacker commands the ranks of the Chaos Space Marines from the Iron Warriors Legion, infiltrating behind the front lines. It cannot include any models with a Wounds characteristic of more than 12, nor any that have the Flyer Battlefield Role.

Each player can include any other models in their army but, if their army is Battle-forged, they will also be able to use the appropriate Stratagems included with this mission (see opposite).

THE BATTLEFIELD

The Defender creates the battlefield, which should have plenty of buildings to represent the hivesprawl. A single building, representing the commander's headquarters, must be set up within the Defender's Command Deployment Zone, as indicated on the map opposite.

DEPLOYMENT

This battle uses the Concealed Deployment rules (see page 194 of *Warhammer 40,000* rulebook). The Defender must set up their Warlord in the headquarters building, and they can only set up units within their Command Deployment Zone that have the HQ, Troops or Elites Battlefield Roles. Any

remaining units must start the battle in the Defender's Front Line Deployment Zone.

Before deploying any models, the Attacker places 3 pseudopod tunnel markers within the Pseudopod Eruption Zone. The centre of each tunnel marker must be at least 12" away from the centre of any other tunnel markers. When deploying units, the Attacker must place them wholly within 6" of any tunnel marker. Any units from the Attacker's army that are not able to be placed on the battlefield are placed in Reserve.

FIRST TURN

The Attacker has the first turn.

UNDERGROUND PASSAGEWAYS

Attacking units that arrive from Reserve must be set up wholly within 6" of any pseudopod tunnel marker, and not within 1" of any enemy units.

RIGID STOICISM

Refusing to desert their post, the Defender's Warlord must remain stationary for the duration of the battle, but the range of that Warlord's Voice of Command ability is increased by 3".

TARGET TERMINATED

If, at any point during the battle, the Defender's Warlord is slain, the battle ends immediately (see Victory Conditions, below).

BATTLE LENGTH

Use the Random Battle Length rules (see page 194 of *Warhammer 40,000* rulebook) to determine how long the battle lasts.

VICTORY CONDITIONS

If, at the end of the battle, the Defender's Warlord has been slain, the Attacker wins a major victory. Any other result is a major victory for the Defender.

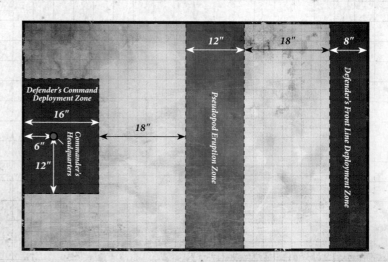

STRATAGEMS

In this mission, the players can use Command Points (CPs) to use the following bonus Stratagems:

2CP TENDRILS OF SCARAX KROND
Attacker Stratagem
The forces of the Iron Warriors pour forth from the giant, cybernetic forelimbs of Etrogar's daemonic forge ship.

Use this Stratagem at the start of your Movement phase. You can place one new pseudopod tunnel marker within the Pseudopod Eruption Zone; the centre of the new tunnel marker must be at least 12" away from the centre of any other tunnel markers. Roll one D6 for each enemy unit within 6" of the new tunnel marker; on a 4+ that unit suffers 1 mortal wound.

1CP FOUL MIASMA
Attacker Stratagem
Choking clouds of industrial waste billow from the vents of snaking pseudopods.

Use this Stratagem at the end of your Movement phase. Select one pseudopod tunnel marker. Until the start of your next Movement phase, units wholly within 6" of that tunnel marker always receive the benefits of cover.

2CP HIDDEN DANGERS
Attacker Stratagem
The tunnels carved out by the arms of the Scarax Krond are filled with hazards and prone to sudden collapse.

Use this Stratagem at the start of your Shooting phase. Select one enemy unit within 2" of a pseudopod tunnel marker. Roll a dice; on a 2+ that unit suffers D3 mortal wounds.

1CP OFF-SITE ARTILLERY
Defender Stratagem
Spying an emerging pseudopod, the hive's defenders are able to target its position with overwhelming firepower.

Use this Stratagem at the start of your opponent's Movement phase. Select one pseudopod tunnel marker. Until the end of the turn, any enemy units that are set up within 6" of that tunnel marker suffer 1 mortal wound.

1CP LEADING BY EXAMPLE
Defender Stratagem
Inspired by their leaders' steadfast refusal to retreat, the beleaguered guardians hold fast.

Use this Stratagem at the start of the Morale phase. Until the end of that phase, friendly **INFANTRY** units can use your Warlord's Leadership characteristic instead of their own whilst they are within 6" of that Warlord.

1CP DETERMINED ADVANCE
Defender Stratagem
The defenders rally with surprising speed, charging back into battle to repel the Chaos assault.

Use this Stratagem in your Movement phase, before making an Advance roll for a unit. When making that Advance roll, roll two D6 and discard a result of your choice when determining the amount that is added to the unit's Movement characteristic.

MISSION VETERANS

In this mission, each player can upgrade one of the units in their army to be a mission veteran. If one player takes a mission veteran, but the other does not have a suitable model, the player without the mission veteran gains 1 additional Command Point at the start of the battle.

ETROGAR'S PROTEGE
Attacker Mission Veteran Stratagem
In the foetid, cloying bowels of the Scarax Krond's forges, the dark Warpsmith shares the rewards of his labours with the most gifted of his aspiring cadre.

Select one **IRON WARRIORS WARPSMITH** model from your army to be one of Etrogar's personal proteges. That model can repair up to two units instead of one, and a unit that was repaired by that model can be repaired for a second time in a turn by that model.

RAPID REACTION FORCE
Defender Mission Veteran Stratagem
The Ghreddask Rapid Reaction Force proved an invaluable aid to the planetary defenders.

Select one **ASTRA MILITARUM VEHICLE** unit from your army to be part of the Ghreddask Rapid Reaction Force. At the start of the first battle round but before the first turn begins, you can move that unit up to 6". It cannot end this move within 9" of any enemy models. If both players have units that can move before the first turn begins, the player who is taking the first turn moves their units first.

ADEPTUS ASTARTES

'I fear that we stand upon the brink of something terrible, brother. The true scale of it yet eludes me, but the signs cannot be ignored. Ultramar must prepare for disaster.'

- *Chief Librarian Tigurius,*
Ultramarines Chapter

MASTERS OF THE CHAPTER

The rules in this section supplement those found in *Codex: Space Marines* and can be used in any open play, narrative play and matched play battles. You'll find Chapter-specific litanies for Chaplains in your Space Marine armies, and a collection of new rules that allow you to represent the upper echelons of a Space Marine Chapter – masters of their associated roles within the Angels of Death.

CHAPTER LITANIES

The page opposite introduces Chapter-specific litanies for your Space Marine Chaplains. These litanies are personal to each Chapter and reflect their background and mentality. Many a Chapter Chaplain will recite these prayers to better imbue their brothers with a fighting spirit.

'In my hands rests the fate, not solely of my Chapter and my brethren, but of scores of worlds. Hundreds. With but a single command I can save a trillion faithful souls, or condemn them to death, or worse. Those who have not carried such a burden cannot imagine its cost. Yet I could not wish for a greater honour. The Emperor forged me for this duty, and I shall never fail him.'

- Chapter Master Eorloid of the Genesis Chapter

CHAPTER COMMAND

This section (pg 33-39) introduces upgrades to various **CHARACTER** models from Space Marine Chapters found in *Codex: Space Marines*. Masters of their craft and leaders of their respective specialisms, they are the upper echelons of the Adeptus Astartes, powerful and influential heroes capable of leading and assisting their brothers in war. For each of the **CHARACTERS** detailed in this section, you will find the following:

STRATAGEMS

If your army is Battle-forged, you have access to a Stratagem that upgrades the specified character to be the leader of their specialism. This character is also given abilities and/or characteristic changes to reflect their substantial experience and influential status. If you have an army roster, specify on it which character(s) you have used these Stratagems on.

WARLORD TRAITS

If your Warlord is a **CHARACTER** that matches the specified Chapter Command keyword, you can give them a Warlord Trait from the appropriate section of this book, instead of one from the *Warhammer 40,000* rulebook or a codex. Named characters have associated Warlord Traits in their codex, and must still take that Warlord Trait.

CHAPTER RELICS

If your army is led by a Space Marines Warlord, you can give one of the Chapter Relics found in the appropriate section of this book to a Space Marine **CHARACTER** from your army that matches the specified Chapter Command keyword. This can be done instead of giving them a Chapter Relic from another source. Named characters and **VEHICLE** models cannot be given any of the Chapter Relics found in this book.

Note that some weapons replace one of the character's existing weapons. Where this is the case, if you are playing a matched play battle, or otherwise using points values, you must still pay the cost of the weapon that is being replaced. Write down any Chapter Relics your models have on your army roster.

CHAPTER LITANIES

Space Marine Chaplains are exemplars of righteous wrath. Powerful orators and accomplished warriors both, they provide bellicose counsel to their comrades and act as spiritual bastions for their Chapter. The litanies that Chaplains intone on the battlefield imbue those around them with fresh determination and martial fury.

If your army is Battle-forged, all **<CHAPTER> CHAPLAINS** (including named characters) in a Space Marines Detachment (other than a Super-heavy Auxiliary Detachment) know litanies from their respective Chapter. This is in addition to any others they know, so long as every unit from that Detachment is drawn from the same Chapter. If your Chaplain is from a successor Chapter and the aforementioned requirements are fulfilled, they know the appropriate Chapter litany from their founding Chapter, and the founding **<CHAPTER>** keyword is replaced with the successor **<CHAPTER>** keyword. For example, if your Chaplain is a **CRIMSON FIST**, he knows the Imperial Fist litany and the **IMPERIAL FISTS** keyword in that litany is replaced with the **CRIMSON FISTS** keyword.

WHITE SCARS: STRIKE OFF THE HEAD

The Chaplain calls his brothers to the hunt and, with prey in their sights, they strike with the savagery of Chogoris.

If this litany is inspiring, then when resolving an attack made with a melee weapon by a model in a friendly **WHITE SCARS** unit within 6" of this model, you can re-roll the wound roll.

IMPERIAL FISTS: FORTRESS OF RESOLVE

The Chaplain retells of the great conflict atop the walls of Terra where stoic resolve was the order of battle amidst a sea of traitors.

If this litany is inspiring, then when resolving an Overwatch attack made by a model in a friendly **IMPERIAL FISTS** unit within 6" of this model, a hit roll of 5 or 6 scores a hit.

SALAMANDERS: SELFLESS SAVIOURS

The Chaplain reminds his brothers of their oaths of guardianship, to think not only of themselves, but also of the protection of their allies.

If this litany is inspiring, friendly **SALAMANDERS** units within 6" of this model can perform Heroic Interventions as if they were a **CHARACTER**.

IRON HANDS: MEDUSAN FURORE

The Chaplain's litany brings forth the slow-building rage exemplified by Ferrus Manus, a dormant volcano that, when unleashed, brings ceaseless destruction.

If this litany is inspiring, add 1 to the Strength characteristic of models in friendly **IRON HANDS** units whilst their unit is within 6" of this model.

ULTRAMARINES: MARCH FOR MACRAGGE

The Chaplain intones the eternal mantra of the Ultramarines.

If this litany is inspiring, then when an Advance roll or Charge roll is made for a friendly **ULTRAMARINES** unit within 6" of this model, you can re-roll any or all dice rolls of 1.

RAVEN GUARD: SWIFT AS THE RAVEN

Whispering softly over the vox, this Chaplain encourages his brothers to remain in motion, not allowing themselves to be tied to a single position.

If this litany is inspiring, select one friendly **RAVEN GUARD** unit within 6" of this model. That unit can shoot in a turn in which it Fell Back. If that unit can **FLY**, it can charge in a turn in which it Fell Back.

MASTER OF SANCTITY

Masters of Sanctity are the High Chaplains of the Space Marine Chapters. They maintain the spiritual well-being of their brothers, ensuring none falter in their responsibilities. Their mere presence inspires fervent aggression amongst their kin, though they are just as capable of delivering retribution first-hand.

STRATAGEMS

If your army is Battle-forged and includes any Space Marines Detachments (excluding Auxiliary Support Detachments), you can use the Stratagem below:

1CP

MASTER OF SANCTITY

Space Marines Stratagem

The greatest amongst the Chaplains is the Master of Sanctity, the spiritual leader of the Chapter. With word and deed he guides his brothers to glory.

Use this Stratagem before the battle. Select one **Chaplain** model from your army that is not a named character. Until the end of the battle, that model gains the **Master of Sanctity** keyword and the following ability: 'Master of Sanctity: This model knows one additional litany from the Litanies of Battle and can recite one additional litany at the start of the battle round'. You can only use this Stratagem once per battle and your army cannot include two **Masters of Sanctity** from the same Chapter.

WARLORD TRAITS

If a **Master of Sanctity** model is your Warlord, you can give them one of the following Warlord Traits:

Wise Orator

A veteran of the battlefield and of the sermon, this Warlord intones his litanies and galvanises his brothers with every word.

When you roll to determine if a litany recited by this Warlord is inspiring, you can re-roll the dice.

Bellowing Firebrand

This Warlord roars his incantations over the din of battle, his thunderous proclamations drowning out the sounds of screams and gunfire.

Add 3" to the range of this Warlord's Spiritual Leader ability and all litanies recited by this Warlord.

RELICS OF THE RECLUSIAM

If your army is led by a Space Marines Warlord, you can give one of the following Chapter Relics to a **Master of Sanctity** model from your army, instead of giving them a Chapter Relic from another source.

Sacrosanct Rosarius

This ancient symbol reflects the Master of Sanctity's station and is an embodiment of that holy office, as well as a powerful force field generator. Blasts of bolter fire and the edges of keen blades alike are deflected in blinding bursts of light. As the bearer advances through the fiercest firestorms unscathed, his brothers are greatly inspired by his apparent invulnerability.

Master of Sanctity model only. A model with this Relic has a 3+ invulnerable save.

The Emperor's Judgement

Legend has it that the golden, skull-faced death mask known as the Emperor's Judgement was crafted in the years following the Horus Heresy, and its crimson, crystal eye lenses are imbued with droplets of his own lifeblood. Regardless of the truth of its origins, several influential Masters of Sanctity have been granted the honour of wearing the Emperor's Judgement in battle. Both heretics and xenos cower in the face of its grim majesty.

Master of Sanctity model only. When resolving an attack made against a model with this Relic, your opponent cannot re-roll the hit roll, your opponent cannot re-roll the wound roll and your opponent cannot re-roll the damage roll. In addition, when a Morale test is taken for an enemy unit within 6" of a model with this Relic, roll two dice and discard the lowest result (if both results are the same, discard either of the dice).

MASTER OF THE FORGE

Masters of the Forge are the chief artificers of Space Marine Chapters. They are responsible for maintaining the arms and armour of their Chapter. Peerless mechanics and technicians, they are the foremost experts within the Adeptus Astartes on the intricacies that surround the machine.

STRATAGEMS

If your army is Battle-forged and includes any Space Marines Detachments (excluding Auxiliary Support Detachments), you can use the Stratagem below:

1CP | MASTER OF THE FORGE
Space Marines Stratagem

Trained on Mars itself, Masters of the Forge are the fathers of the forge and the custodians of the machine. They oversee the Chapter's Armoury and know the intimate workings of its parts.

Use this Stratagem before the battle. Select one **Techmarine** model from your army that is not a named character or a **Techmarine Gunner**. Until the end of the battle, that model gains the **Master of the Forge** keyword and the following ability: 'Master of the Forge: When this model repairs a model using its Blessing of the Omnissiah ability, that model regains up to 3 lost wounds instead of up to D3'. You can only use this Stratagem once per battle and your army cannot include two **Masters of the Forge** from the same Chapter.

WARLORD TRAITS

If a **Master of the Forge** model is your Warlord, you can give them one of the following Warlord Traits:

Master the Machine

This Warlord is attuned to the machine spirit like no other, and can conduct his charges meticulously to bring ruin to their enemies.

When resolving an attack made by a friendly **<Chapter> Vehicle** model within 6" of this Warlord, add 1 to the hit roll.

Warden of the Ancients

This Warlord has an affinity with the Dreadnoughts of his Chapter. He meticulously tends to his bellicose, ill-tempered charges, ensuring that when the time comes for them to take to the battlefield, they fight with unrivalled fury.

Add 1 to the Strength and Attacks characteristics of friendly **<Chapter> Dreadnought** models whilst they are within 6" of this Warlord.

RELICS OF THE FORGE

If your army is led by a Space Marines Warlord, you can give one of the following Chapter Relics to a **Master of the Forge** model from your army, instead of giving them a Chapter Relic from another source.

Mortis Machina

Forged deep within the subterranean vaults of holy Mars, this master-crafted power axe hews through not just the metal armour of war engines and vehicles, but through their very machine spirit. Even a glancing blow can gut an enemy tank or walker.

Master of the Forge model with power axe only. This relic replaces a model's power axe and has the following profile:

WEAPON	RANGE	TYPE	S	AP	D
Mortis Machina	Melee	Melee	+3	-3	D3

Abilities: When resolving an attack made with this weapon against a **Vehicle** unit, if the saving throw is failed that unit suffers 1 mortal wound in addition to any other damage.

The Endurant Protector

The Endurant Protector was crafted by a long-forgotten Master of the Forge, and consists of an adamantium and electrum carapace, beautifully engraved with runic wards and oaths of eternal vigilance. The Protector has been tested in countless war zones and has never been found wanting. The fires of war have scorched its surface over and over, yet at battle's end its current bearer returns to the forge to repair the ancient relic, tempering and strengthening its impenetrable surface in the process.

Master of the Forge model only. Add 1 to the Toughness characteristic of a model with this Relic. A model with this Relic has a 4+ invulnerable save.

CHIEF LIBRARIAN

Chief Librarians are the masters of Space Marine Chapters' Librarius. Battle scholars with vast experience and immense psychic power, they are as much invaluable warriors as they are dependable advisors. When mastery of the warp is required, none are better equipped to deal with its turbulent nature.

STRATAGEMS

If your army is Battle-forged and includes any Space Marines Detachments (excluding Auxiliary Support Detachments), you can use the Stratagem below:

1CP — CHIEF LIBRARIAN
Space Marines Stratagem

As masters of the psychic arts, Chief Librarians can direct the energies of the immaterium with unrivalled precision and power.

Use this Stratagem before the battle. Select one **Librarian** model from your army that is not a named character. Until the end of the battle, that model gains the **Chief Librarian** keyword and the following ability: '**Chief Librarian**: This model knows one additional psychic power from their chosen discipline and can attempt to Deny one additional psychic power in your opponent's Psychic phase'. You can only use this Stratagem once per battle and your army cannot include two **Chief Librarians** from the same Chapter.

WARLORD TRAITS

If a **Chief Librarian Character** model is your Warlord, you can give them one of the following Warlord Traits:

Psychic Mastery

This Warlord has reached a level of psychic mastery that allows him to delve deep into the warp, to depths that would cause lesser psykers to be consumed by its ravenous energies.

When a Psychic test is taken for this Warlord for the first time in a phase, add 1 to the total.

High Scholar of the Librarius

This Warlord is the keeper of the Chapter's most ancient texts, a learned scholar with unparalleled empyric knowledge.

This Warlord can generate psychic powers from any discipline that they can know powers from (rather than generating psychic powers from only one discipline).

RELICS OF THE LIBRARIUS

If your army is led by a Space Marines Warlord, you can give one of the following Chapter Relics to a **Chief Librarian** model from your army, instead of giving them a Chapter Relic from another source.

VINCULUM VITAE

An incredibly powerful and dangerous artefact, the sword known as the Vinculum Vitae was recovered from the battlefield of Eonis Verge, in which seven Chief Librarians from multiple Chapters united to banish a horde of Tzeentch Daemons – giving their lives in the process. Imbued with the terrible, psychic echoes of that engagement, the Vinculum Vitae unleashes a torrent of catastrophic energy with each blow.

Model with force sword only. This Relic replaces a force sword and has the following profile:

WEAPON	RANGE	TYPE	S	AP	D
Vinculum Vitae	Melee	Melee	+1	-3	D3

Abilities: When resolving an attack made with this weapon, an unmodified wound roll of 6 inflicts D3 mortal wounds on the target instead of any other damage.

NEURAL SHROUD

The Neural Shroud is a specially modified psychic hood sometimes worn by the most senior members of a Chapter's Librarius. The resonating crystals within its neurokinetic housing have been supercharged with empyric energy. Though wearing such a potent device demands incredible focus and willpower, it projects an extremely potent anti-psychic field.

Add 12" to the range of a model with this Relic's Psychic Hood ability.

CHIEF APOTHECARY

Chief Apothecaries are the most senior surgeons and battle medics available to Space Marine Chapters. Calm and resolute, they maintain the life force of their battle-brothers on and off the battlefield. Most importantly, they are responsible for their Chapter's future in the preservation of Space Marine gene-seed.

STRATAGEMS

If your army is Battle-forged and includes any Space Marines Detachments (excluding Auxiliary Support Detachments), you can use the Stratagem below:

1CP | **CHIEF APOTHECARY**
Space Marines Stratagem

With vast experience to draw upon, a Chapter's Chief Apothecary is its ultimate practitioner of the healer's art.

Use this Stratagem before the battle. Select one **APOTHECARY** model from your army that is not a named character. Until the end of the battle, that model gains the **CHIEF APOTHECARY** keyword and the following ability: 'Chief Apothecary: When this model provides medical attention to a unit, you can re-roll the dice to determine if a destroyed model is returned to that unit'. You can only use this Stratagem once per battle once and your army cannot include two **CHIEF APOTHECARIES** from the same Chapter.

WARLORD TRAITS

If a **CHIEF APOTHECARY** model is your Warlord, you can give them one of the following Warlord Traits:

FATHER OF THE FUTURE

With this custodian at their side, battle-brothers fight without restraint, safe in the knowledge that their legacy, and that of their Chapter, is secured.

When a model in a friendly <**CHAPTER**> **INFANTRY** or <**CHAPTER**> **BIKER** unit would lose a wound whilst their unit is within 6" of this Warlord, roll one D6; on a 6, that wound is not lost. If that unit has the Flesh is Weak Chapter Tactic, that wound is not lost on a 5+ instead.

SELFLESS HEALER

This Warlord moves across the battlefield swiftly and purposefully to heal his brothers.

This Warlord can provide medical attention to up to two units instead of one, and a unit that was provided medical attention by this Warlord can be provided with medical attention for a second time in a turn by this Warlord. Note that this Warlord can do so even if it is recovering the gene-seed of a fallen warrior.

RELICS OF THE APOTHECARIUM

If your army is led by a Space Marines Warlord, you can give one of the following Chapter Relics to a **CHIEF APOTHECARY** model from your army, instead of giving them a Chapter Relic from another source.

ACQUITTAL

Acquittal is a master-crafted absolvor bolt pistol, equipped with a powerful bio-auspex scope. This allows the wielder to both dispatch his foes with surgical precision, and distribute swift and painless oblivion to his wounded battle-brothers.

Model with bolt pistol or absolvor bolt pistol only. This Relic replaces a bolt pistol or absolvor pistol and has the following profile:

WEAPON	RANGE	TYPE	S	AP	D
Acquittal	16"	Pistol 1	5	-3	1

Abilities: When resolving an attack made with this weapon against a unit that is not a **VEHICLE** or **MONSTER**, this weapon has a Damage characteristic of D6 for that attack.

HEALER'S AEGIS

The Healer's Aegis is a sophisticated adaption of the refractor fields common to many officers of the Imperium. The projected energy field is extended to protect not only the Chief Apothecary, but those in his care. Even as he performs intricate and bloody battlefield surgery, the Apothecary can position himself to protect nearby brothers.

Friendly <**CHAPTER**> **INFANTRY** models have a 5+ invulnerable save whilst they are within 1" of a model with this Relic.

CHAPTER ANCIENT

Only the most distinguished Space Marines are granted the title of Chapter Ancient. Given the sacred task of bearing the Chapter's standard to war, they selflessly fly the colours even as they slay their foes. The sight of such a holy relic flying high above the battlefield inspires the Ancients' brethren to give their all.

STRATAGEMS

If your army is Battle-forged and includes any Space Marines Detachments (excluding Auxiliary Support Detachments), you can use the Stratagem below:

CHAPTER ANCIENT
1CP

Space Marines Stratagem

The mere presence of the Chapter's standard is worth a fortified bastion to the warriors of the Adeptus Astartes.

Use this Stratagem before the battle. Select one **ANCIENT** model from your army that is not a named character. Add 1 to the Leadership characteristic of that model. In addition, that model gains the **CHAPTER ANCIENT** keyword and the following ability: 'Chapter Banner: Friendly **<CHAPTER>** units benefit from this model's Astartes Banner ability if they are within 9" of it instead of 6". You can only use this Stratagem once per battle and your army cannot include two **CHAPTER ANCIENTS** from the same Chapter.

WARLORD TRAITS

If a **CHAPTER ANCIENT** model is your Warlord, you can give them one of the following Warlord Traits:

SINGULAR PRESENCE

When this Warlord takes to the field it unifies his brothers, his battle honours and accomplishments standing as an example to all.

Friendly **<CHAPTER> INFANTRY**, **<CHAPTER> BIKER** and **<CHAPTER> DREADNOUGHT** units within 3" of this Warlord can perform Heroic Interventions as if they were **CHARACTERS**.

STEADFAST EXAMPLE

This Warlord vows to secure victory no matter the cost, and inspires his brethren to take a similar oath.

Friendly **<CHAPTER> INFANTRY** units have the Defenders of Humanity ability (see *Codex: Space Marines*) whilst they are within 3" of this Warlord. If such a unit already has this ability, each model counts as one additional model when determining control of an objective marker.

BANNERS OF THE CHAPTER

If your army is led by a Space Marines Warlord, you can give one of the following Chapter Relics to a **CHAPTER ANCIENT** model from your army, instead of giving them a Chapter Relic from another source.

STANDARD OF RIGHTEOUS HATRED

Rather than a glorious recounting of the Chapter's triumphs, emblazoned upon this bloodstained banner are accounts of the atrocities and injustices committed by its foes, a reminder of the sacred duty of the Adeptus Astartes to purge the stars of the heretic and the alien.

Model with the Astartes Banner ability only. A model with this Relic has the following additional ability:

Standard of Righteous Hatred: Models that shoot with one of their ranged weapons, or make a single attack with one of their melee weapons, as a result of this model's Astartes Banner ability always resolve their attack as if they had a Ballistic Skill and Weapon Skill characteristic of 2+.

PENNANT OF THE FALLEN

This hallowed standard records the names of legendary Space Marines of the Chapter, mighty heroes who have fallen in glorious battle against the xenos and the heretic. The last stands of these warriors are mighty tales of defiance in the face of overwhelming odds. Warring under the shadow of such a proud legacy inspires battle-brothers to fight until their final breath.

Model with the Astartes Banner ability only. The banner grants the bearer the following additional ability:

Pennant of the Fallen: **<CHAPTER>** models that attack with one of their melee weapons as a result of this model's Astartes Banner ability can make two attacks instead of one.

CHAPTER CHAMPION

The honorific of Chapter Champion is bestowed upon Space Marine Chapters' mightiest warriors. These martial masters fight for the glory and honour of their battle-brothers. In combat, they will seek out worthy warriors and warlords to cross blades with, and can single-handedly turn the tide of conflict.

STRATAGEMS

If your army is Battle-forged and includes any Space Marines Detachments (excluding Auxiliary Support Detachments), you can use the Stratagem below:

1CP

CHAPTER CHAMPION
Space Marines Stratagem

Only the most noble and accomplished of warriors ascend to this rank, the shining example of a Chapter's glory and martial capabilities.

Use this Stratagem before the battle. Select one **COMPANY CHAMPION** model from your army that is not a named character. Until the end of the battle, that model's Attacks and Leadership characteristics are increased by 1, and it gains the **CHAPTER CHAMPION** keyword and the following ability: 'Skilful Parry': When resolving an attack made with a melee weapon against this model, subtract 1 from the hit roll'. You can only use this Stratagem once per battle and your army cannot include two **CHAPTER CHAMPIONS** from the same Chapter.

WARLORD TRAITS

If a **CHAPTER CHAMPION** model is your Warlord, you can give them one of the following Warlord Traits:

MASTER DUELLIST

This warrior is an unparalleled duellist who delivers strikes and ripostes with lethal precision.

When resolving an attack made with a melee weapon by a model against this Warlord, on a hit roll of 1 roll one D6; on a 4+ that model's unit suffers 1 mortal wound after that unit has finished shooting or fighting.

MARTIAL EXEMPLAR

This warlord is an exquisite warrior whose deeds inspire those around him. His swift advances galvanise his brothers for the honour of fighting beside an exemplar of the Chapter.

When a charge roll is made for a friendly <**CHAPTER**> unit within 6" of this Warlord, you can re-roll the roll.

RELICS OF THE CHAPTER

If your army is led by a Space Marines Warlord, you can give one of the following Chapter Relics to a **CHAPTER CHAMPION** model from your army, instead of giving them a Chapter Relic from another source.

BLADE OF TRIUMPH

This gleaming broadsword is a masterpiece of artifice and a weapon befitting any Chapter Champion. Its perfectly weighted blade is etched with the names of its previous wielders and a catalogue of their most magnificent deeds. By pressing an indentation in the sword's electrum grip the wielder can overcharge its power field with a surge of fiery energy, allowing the Blade of Triumph to cleave through the thickest armour.

Model with master-crafted power sword only. This Relic replaces a master-crafted power sword and has the following profile:

WEAPON	RANGE	TYPE	S	AP	D
Blade of Triumph	Melee	Melee	+2	-4	3

THE ANGEL ARTIFICE

The surface of this exquisite battle plate is woven with a mysterious, super-dense alloy, the exact nature of which has been lost to history. Whatever its origin, it absorbs and refracts incoming energy, rendering the wearer all but invulnerable. Such a priceless relic is bestowed upon only the greatest heroes of the Adeptus Astartes.

A model with this Relic has a Save characteristic of 2+ and a 4+ invulnerable save.

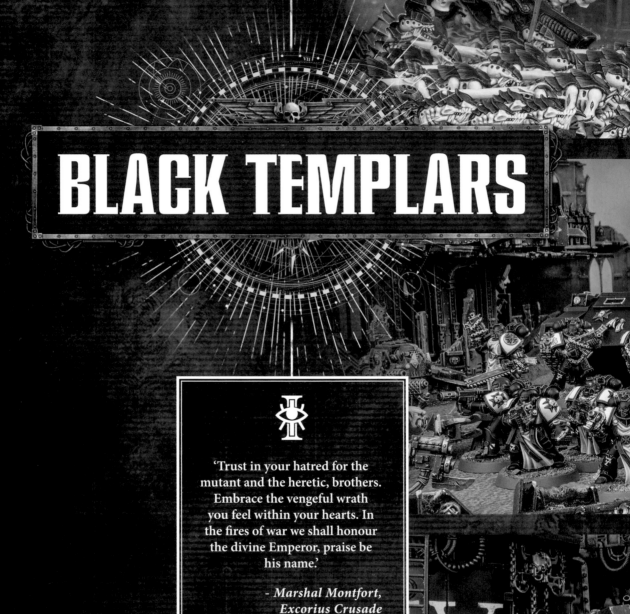

BLACK TEMPLARS

'Trust in your hatred for the mutant and the heretic, brothers. Embrace the vengeful wrath you feel within your hearts. In the fires of war we shall honour the divine Emperor, praise be his name.'

- Marshal Montfort,
Excorius Crusade

HEROES OF THE BLACK TEMPLARS

The battle-brothers of the Black Templars stand apart from their fellow Space Marines, for they accept the divinity of the God-Emperor as holy truth. Pious, aggressive warrior-knights, they roam across the galaxy in great crusade fleets, laying waste to aliens and heretics wherever they are found.

One of the Imperial Fists' first successor Chapters, the Black Templars have since become one of the largest and most feared Space Marine Chapters. The first High Marshal of the Black Templars – the legendary Sigismund – refused to adhere to the Codex Astartes, seeing the foundational treatise written by Roboute Guilliman as an insult to the teachings of his own Primarch, Rogal Dorn. Instead, he led his warriors into the depths of space, taking the war directly to the enemies of the Imperium. In the centuries since, the Chapter has diverted even further from the tenets of the Adeptus Astartes.

Embracing their faith and acknowledging the God-Emperor's divinity, the Black Templars have developed a fanatical zealotry and aggressiveness. This deviation from orthodoxy disturbs many of their fellow Space Marine Chapters, though the Black Templars' dedication to eradicating the enemies of Humanity cannot be questioned.

The Black Templars are a fleet-based Chapter and claim no single home world as their own. Instead, their enormous armadas can be found across the galaxy. The Black Templars refuse to adhere

to the limit of one thousand Space Marines per Chapter, set out in the Codex Astartes. Each of their crusades is comprised of thousands of Space Marines, though the current High Marshal, Helbrecht, maintains overall authority from the deck of his battle barge, the *Eternal Crusader*.

As befits the heirs of the legendary swordsman Sigismund, the Black Templars are specialists in the white-hot fury of close combat. They launch themselves upon the enemy with a merciless, focused aggression, bellowing battle-oaths as they carve their foes apart. They carry a particularly intense hatred for xenos witchkin and rogue psykers, and will purge these hated foes wherever they are found.

HIGH MARSHAL HELBRECHT

High Marshal Helbrecht exemplifies the hallmark qualities of the Black Templars – stubbornness, personal honour, and unswerving loyalty to the Emperor. His rise through the Chapter was swift, impressing his peers with the sheer ferocity of his desire to slay the enemies of the Emperor. Even as an Initiate, Helbrecht fought with zeal and courage beyond expectation. He held the line against a vast swarm of Tyranids at Deathcore Ridge, and refused to yield whilst there yet remained a foe to fight. Helbrecht was inducted into the Sword Brethren just a few decades later, for the legendary feat of besting a Daemon Prince with only his combat blade. After this, his meteoric ascension continued apace, paved at every step with the deaths of the Emperor's most fearsome enemies. When High Marshal

Kordhel was slain by a frenzied Berzerker, the Marshals of the Black Templars gathered to choose a new leader for their Chapter. Helbrecht was elected unanimously and presented with the Sword of the High Marshals.

CHAPLAIN GRIMALDUS

Grimaldus is a veteran of centuries of combat, but only in the past few decades has he borne the mantle of the Black Templars' High Chaplain. It is a responsibility that weighs greatly upon Grimaldus' shoulders, and he constantly strives to prove that he is worthy of the honour.

Grimaldus' trial by fire as High Chaplain was the Third War for Armageddon. With High Marshal Helbrecht combating the Orks in space, it fell to Grimaldus to lead the Black Templars' ground forces. During the Battle for Hive Helsreach, Grimaldus faced what seemed like certain death against successive hordes of Orks. Only the High Chaplain's iron resolve and deadly combat skills saw him through the apocalyptic battle that followed, earning him great renown.

Ever since, Grimaldus has been a rallying point for the Black Templars. Even before the war ended, the citizens of Hive Helsreach honoured him with the title of Hero of Helsreach, and bowed before his passing. No battle is so bleak that his appearance cannot turn the tide and rekindle the fire in his brothers' hearts.

THE EMPEROR'S CHAMPION

At the forefront of the Black Templars' battle line strides a singular figure, his gleaming Black Sword carving a path of ruin through the foe. This warrior will challenge any enemy, no matter how mighty, for he is the Emperor's Champion. Divinity rests upon his shoulders as both mantle and shroud, though whispers from some who have fought alongside the Emperor's Champion say he walks in shadow, half-possessed by visitations of a supernatural vengeance.

When battle is joined, divine might flows through the Emperor's Champion's every sinew. His vision shimmers with golden light that burns brightest around the mightiest of enemies. He charges through the press, slashing lesser enemies aside as he closes upon his target. Leaving his brethren to fight the broader battle, the Emperor's Champion uses precision and surety to cut down those who would challenge the supremacy of Mankind.

CRUSADER SQUADS

The majority of Black Templars battle-brothers – known within the Chapter as Initiates – are organised into Crusader Squads, which form the backbone of any strike force. Many Crusader Squads have the honour of being led to battle by one of the Chapter's Sword Brethren, veterans whose deeds inspire the Initiates to ever greater acts of courage. Crusader Squads are armed primarily with the holy bolter, though Black Templars prefer to fight their foes face-to-face. Many choose to carry chainswords, or other weapons more suited to close combat. Crusader Squads epitomise the Black Templars' righteous zeal, and their drive to defeat their foes in battle.

Rather than fielding a dedicated Scout Company, Black Templars Neophytes are inducted directly into the Crusader Squads. There, they learn to master the blade and bolter under the guidance of their Initiate battle-brothers.

'By our blades will the xenos canker be excised from the galaxy. By our flamers will the heretic and the traitor be consumed in the fires of damnation. We are the Emperor's final word to all who would deny Humanity's divine mandate; vengeance is coming.'

- Chaplain Grimaldus, Litanies of Hate

ZEALOUS CRUSADERS

In this section you will find the datasheets and points values for the BLACK TEMPLARS units described in this book, and rules for Battle-forged armies that include Black Templars Detachments – that is, Detachments that only include BLACK TEMPLARS units. These include a series of Warlord Traits, a name generator, Stratagems, Chapter Relics, litanies and Tactical Objectives. Together, these reflect the character and fighting style of the Black Templars in your games of Warhammer 40,000.

CODEX SUPPLEMENT

This section is a supplement to *Codex: Space Marines* – you will need a copy of that book to use the rules and datasheets in this section. Wargear lists, the Angels of Death ability, a definition of bolt weapons, the Litanies of Battle and more can all be found within the pages of *Codex: Space Marines*.

ABILITIES

If your army is Battle-forged, all units from your army with the Combat Doctrines ability (see *Codex: Space Marines*) gain the Knights of Sigismund ability, so long as every unit from your army (with the exception of those that are UNALIGNED) are BLACK TEMPLARS.

KNIGHTS OF SIGISMUND

Skilled with both blade and bolter in equal measure, the warriors of the Black Templars are a creed unto themselves. A brethren of unquestioning loyalty, they exist to bring the Emperor's retribution to every heretic and unbeliever within the Imperium and beyond.

Whilst the Assault Doctrine is active, when resolving an attack made with a melee weapon by a BLACK TEMPLARS model with this ability against a unit that is not a VEHICLE in a turn in which that model made a charge move or performed a Heroic Intervention, an unmodified hit roll of 6 automatically scores a hit and successfully wounds the target (do not make a wound roll).

THE LOST LIBRARIUS

It is uncertain how, or when, the Black Templars ceased to field Librarians. Whatever the reason, they now wage war without these powerful warriors.

LIBRARIAN units cannot be from the BLACK TEMPLARS Chapter.

CHOSEN CHAMPION

On the eve of battle, as the Black Templars gather to hear the benedictions of the faithful, one among them may be chosen by the divine to bear the mantle of the Emperor's Champion in the coming conflict.

The Chapter Champion Stratagem (pg 39) cannot be used to affect BLACK TEMPLARS units.

HIGH MARSHAL HELBRECHT

NAME	M	WS	BS	S	T	W	A	Ld	Sv
High Marshal Helbrecht	6"	2+	2+	4	4	6	5	9	2+

High Marshal Helbrecht is a single model equipped with: combi-melta; Sword of the High Marshals; frag grenades; krak grenades. You can only include one of this model in your army.

WEAPON	RANGE	TYPE	S	AP	D	ABILITIES
Combi-melta	When you choose this weapon to shoot with, select one or both of the profiles below. If you select both, subtract 1 from hit rolls for attacks made with this weapon.					
- Boltgun	24"	Rapid Fire 1	4	0	1	-
- Meltagun	12"	Assault 1	8	-4	D6	When resolving an attack made with this weapon against a unit that is within half range, roll two D6 when inflicting damage with it and discard one of the results.
Sword of the High Marshals	Melee	Melee	+1	-3	D3	When the bearer fights in a turn in which it made a charge move or performed a Heroic Intervention, it makes D3 additional attacks with this weapon.
Frag grenades	6"	Grenade D6	3	0	1	-
Krak grenades	6"	Grenade 1	6	-1	D3	

ABILITIES	**Angels of Death** (see *Codex: Space Marines*) **Chapter Master:** You can re-roll hit rolls for attacks made by models in friendly **Black Templars** units whilst their unit is within 6" of this model.	**Crusade of Wrath:** Add 1 to the Strength characteristic of friendly **Black Templars** models whilst their unit is within 6" of this model. **Iron Halo:** This model has a 4+ invulnerable save.
FACTION KEYWORDS	IMPERIUM, ADEPTUS ASTARTES, BLACK TEMPLARS	
KEYWORDS	CHARACTER, INFANTRY, CHAPTER MASTER, HIGH MARSHAL HELBRECHT	

With a glorious history and impeccable battle record, the Black Templars follow High Marshal Helbrecht into the most terrible battles without hesitation, knowing that they cannot lose.

THE EMPEROR'S CHAMPION

NAME	M	WS	BS	S	T	W	A	Ld	Sv
The Emperor's Champion	6"	2+	3+	4	4	4	5	9	2+

The Emperor's Champion is a single model equipped with: bolt pistol; Black Sword; frag grenades; krak grenades. You can only include one of this model in your army.

WEAPON	RANGE	TYPE	S	AP	D	ABILITIES
Bolt pistol	12"	Pistol 1	4	0	1	-
Black Sword	Melee	Melee	+2	-3	D3	When resolving an attack made with this weapon against a **CHARACTER** or **MONSTER** unit, you can re-roll the wound roll.
Frag grenades	6"	Grenade D6	3	0	1	-
Krak grenades	6"	Grenade 1	6	-1	D3	-

ABILITIES	
Angels of Death (see *Codex: Space Marines*) **Sigismund's Honour:** Add 1 to this model's Strength and Attacks characteristics whilst it is within 1" of any enemy **CHARACTER** models. **Skilful Parry:** When resolving an attack made with a melee weapon against this model, subtract 1 from the hit roll.	**Slayer of Champions:** When resolving an attack made with a melee weapon by this model against an enemy **CHARACTER** unit, you can re-roll the hit roll. **Armour of Faith:** This model has a 4+ invulnerable save.

FACTION KEYWORDS	**IMPERIUM, ADEPTUS ASTARTES, BLACK TEMPLARS**
KEYWORDS	**CHARACTER, INFANTRY, EMPEROR'S CHAMPION**

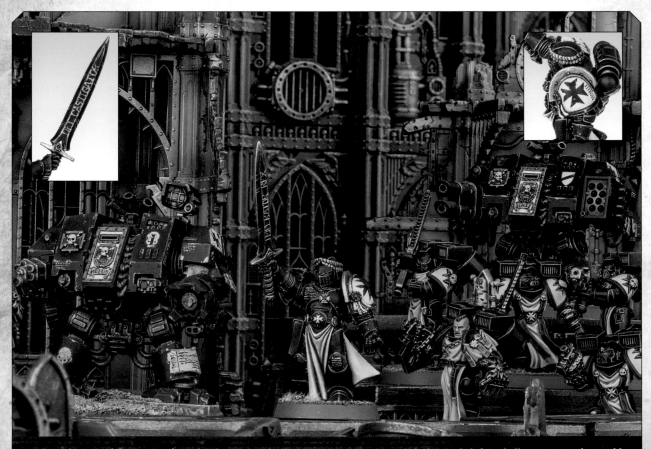

A living beacon of the Emperor's might, the Emperor's Champion raises the shining Black Sword aloft in challenge to any who would dare stand against the wrath of the Black Templars.

CHAPLAIN GRIMALDUS

NAME	M	WS	BS	S	T	W	A	Ld	Sv
Chaplain Grimaldus	6"	2+	3+	4	4	4	3	9	3+

Chaplain Grimaldus is a single model equipped with: plasma pistol; artificer crozius; frag grenades; krak grenades. You can only include one of this model in your army.

WEAPON	RANGE	TYPE	S	AP	D	ABILITIES
Plasma pistol	When you choose this weapon to shoot with, select one of the profiles below.					
- Standard	12"	Pistol 1	7	-3	1	-
- Supercharge	12"	Pistol 1	8	-3	2	If any hit rolls of 1 are made for attacks with this weapon, the bearer is destroyed after shooting with this weapon.
Artificer crozius	Melee	Melee	+2	-2	2	-
Frag grenades	6"	Grenade D6	3	0	1	-
Krak grenades	6"	Grenade 1	6	-1	D3	-

ABILITIES	**Angels of Death** (see *Codex: Space Marines*) **Spiritual Leader:** Friendly **BLACK TEMPLARS** units can use this model's Leadership characteristic instead of their own whilst they are within 6" of this model. **Devout Puritan:** This model can attempt to resist one psychic power in your opponent's Psychic phase in the same manner as a **PSYKER** by taking a Deny the Witch test.	**Unmatched Zeal:** When resolving an attack made with a melee weapon by a model in a friendly **BLACK TEMPLARS** unit within 6" of this model, on an unmodified hit roll of 6 you can make 1 additional attack against the same unit using the same weapon. This additional attack cannot generate another attack. **Rosarius:** This model has a 4+ invulnerable save.
PRIEST	This model knows the Litany of Hate (see below) and either two litanies from the Litanies of Battle (see *Codex: Space Marines*) or two litanies from the Litanies of the Devout (pg 49). At the start of the battle round, this model can recite two litanies it knows that have not already been recited by a friendly model that battle round. Roll one D6; on a 3+ the recited litany is inspiring and takes effect until the end of that battle round. **Litany of Hate:** If this litany is inspiring, you can re-roll hit rolls for attacks made with melee weapons by models in friendly **BLACK TEMPLARS** units whilst their unit is within 6" of this model.	
FACTION KEYWORDS	IMPERIUM, ADEPTUS ASTARTES, BLACK TEMPLARS	
KEYWORDS	CHARACTER, INFANTRY, PRIEST, MASTER OF SANCTITY, CHAPLAIN, GRIMALDUS	

CENOBYTE SERVITORS

NAME	M	WS	BS	S	T	W	A	Ld	Sv
Cenobyte Servitor	5"	5+	5+	3	3	1	1	6	4+

This unit contains 3 Cenobyte Servitors. Every model is equipped with: close combat weapon. You can only include one of this unit in your army.

WEAPON	RANGE	TYPE	S	AP	D	ABILITIES
Close combat weapon	Melee	Melee	User	0	1	-

ABILITIES	**Mindwiped:** Models in this unit have Weapon Skill and Ballistic Skill characteristics of 4+, and a Leadership characteristic of 9, whilst their unit is within 6" of **CHAPLAIN GRIMALDUS**. **Chaplain's Retinue:** If your army is Battle-forged, this unit does not take up slots in a Detachment that includes **CHAPLAIN GRIMALDUS**.	**Relic of Helsreach:** When a model in a friendly **BLACK TEMPLARS** unit that is within 6" of this unit would lose a wound as a result of a mortal wound, roll one D6; on a 4+ that wound is not lost. This is not cumulative with any other rules that allow a model to not lose wounds as a result of a mortal wound.
FACTION KEYWORDS	IMPERIUM, ADEPTUS ASTARTES, BLACK TEMPLARS	
KEYWORDS	INFANTRY, SERVITORS, CENOBYTE SERVITORS	

CRUSADER SQUAD

NAME	M	WS	BS	S	T	W	A	Ld	Sv
Initiate	6"	3+	3+	4	4	1	1	7	3+
Neophyte	6"	3+	3+	4	4	1	1	6	4+
Sword Brother	6"	3+	3+	4	4	1	2	8	3+

This unit contains 1 Sword Brother and 4 Initiates. It can additionally contain up to 5 Initiates (**Power Rating +4**). It can additionally contain up to 5 Neophytes (**Power Rating +3**) or up to 10 Neophytes (**Power Rating +6**). Every model is equipped with: bolt pistol; boltgun; frag grenades; krak grenades.

WEAPON	RANGE	TYPE	S	AP	D	ABILITIES
Astartes shotgun	12"	Assault 2	4	0	1	When resolving an attack made with this weapon against a unit that is within half range, this weapon has a Strength characteristic of 5.
Bolt pistol	12"	Pistol 1	4	0	1	-
Boltgun	24"	Rapid Fire 1	4	0	1	-
Chainsword	Melee	Melee	User	0	1	When the bearer fights, it can make 1 additional attack with this weapon.
Combat knife	Melee	Melee	User	0	1	When the bearer fights, it can make 1 additional attack with this weapon.
Power axe	Melee	Melee	+1	-2	1	-
Power fist	Melee	Melee	x2	-3	D3	When attacking with this weapon, you must subtract 1 from the hit roll.
Power maul	Melee	Melee	+2	-1	1	-
Power sword	Melee	Melee	User	-3	1	-
Frag grenades	6"	Grenade D6	3	0	1	-
Krak grenades	6"	Grenade 1	6	-1	D3	-

WARGEAR OPTIONS	
	• Any Initiate can be equipped with 1 chainsword instead of 1 boltgun.
	• Any Neophyte can be equipped with one of the following instead of 1 boltgun: 1 Astartes shotgun; 1 combat knife.
	• If this unit contains fewer than 10 models, 1 Initiate can be equipped with one of the following instead of a 1 boltgun: 1 power axe; 1 power fist; 1 power maul; 1 power sword; 1 weapon from the *Heavy Weapons* list; 1 weapon from the *Special Weapons* list.
	• If this unit contains 10 or more models, 1 Initiate can be equipped with 1 weapon from the *Special Weapons* list instead of 1 boltgun, and 1 Initiate can be equipped with one of the following instead of 1 boltgun: 1 power axe; 1 power fist; 1 power maul; 1 power sword; 1 weapon from the *Heavy Weapons* list.
	• The Sword Brother can be equipped with up to 2 weapons from the *Sergeant Weapons* list instead of 1 bolt pistol and 1 boltgun.

ABILITIES	
	Angels of Death (see *Codex: Space Marines*)
	Paired Combatants: Whilst this unit contains at least as many Initiates as Neophytes, when resolving an attack made with a melee weapon by a Neophyte in this unit, re-roll a hit roll of 1.

FACTION KEYWORDS	**IMPERIUM, ADEPTUS ASTARTES, BLACK TEMPLARS**
KEYWORDS	**INFANTRY, CRUSADER SQUAD**

LITANIES OF THE DEVOUT

Unlike the majority of Adeptus Astartes Chapters, the Black Templars maintain an unwavering belief in the Emperor of Mankind's divinity. As a result, the litanies of Black Templars Chaplains are designed to stir the furious zealotry of their battle-brothers.

A **Black Templars Chaplain** model in a **Black Templars** Detachment can know litanies from the Litanies of the Devout, instead of knowing litanies from the Litanies of Battle (see *Codex: Space Marines*). A **Black Templars Chaplain** model that does generates an equivalent number of litanies from the Litanies of the Devout (they cannot generate litanies from more than one litany table). You can either roll one D6 to generate each litany randomly (re-rolling duplicate results), or you can select which litanies the model knows.

D6 LITANY

1 LITANY OF DIVINE PROTECTION

The Chaplain rouses the ardent souls of his brothers, calling upon the godly essence of the Emperor to shield his sons from the blasphemy of the unbeliever.

If this litany is inspiring, select one friendly **Black Templars** unit within 6" of this model. When a model in that unit would lose a wound, roll one D6; on a 5+ that wound is not lost.

2 PSALM OF REMORSELESS PERSECUTION

4 FIRES OF DEVOTION

The Chaplain's words speak to the very souls of his battle-brothers, enflaming them with ardour and their blade arms with divine strength.

If this litany is inspiring, select one friendly **Black Templars** unit within 6" of this model. If that unit makes a charge move or performs a Heroic Intervention, add 1 to the Attacks characteristic of models in that unit until the end of the turn.

5 FERVENT ACCLAMATION

WARLORD TRAITS

If a **BLACK TEMPLARS CHARACTER** model is your Warlord, you can use the Black Templars Warlord Traits table below to determine what Warlord Trait they have. You can either roll one D6 on the table below to randomly generate a Warlord Trait, or you can select the one that best suits your Warlord's preferred style of waging war.

D6 WARLORD TRAIT

1 OATHKEEPER

The fury of a Black Templars warlord cannot be stayed until the foe lies ruined at his feet.

This Warlord can perform a Heroic Intervention if there are any enemy units within 6" of them instead of 3", and when doing so can move up to 6" instead of 3".

2 EPITOME OF PIETY

So intense is the warlord's devotion to the God-Emperor that they are able to throw off the malign influence of the warp.

This Warlord can attempt to resist one psychic power in your opponent's Psychic phase in the same manner as a **PSYKER** by taking a Deny the Witch test. When a Deny the Witch test is taken for this Warlord, add 1 to the total.

3 PARAGON OF FURY

This warlord's hatred for the heretic and the unbeliever burns with the fury of a newborn star.

After this Warlord finishes a charge move, for each enemy unit within 1" of this Warlord roll one D6; on a 2+ that unit suffers 1 mortal wound.

4 MASTER OF ARMS

The warlord has devoted their existence to the rigorous perfection of both blade and bolter, becoming a force of righteous destruction upon the battlefield.

This Warlord always fights first in the Fight phase, even if they did not charge. If the enemy has units that have charged, or that have a similar ability, then alternate choosing units to fight with, starting with the player whose turn is taking place.

5 INSPIRATIONAL FIGHTER

The warlord's exemplary martial prowess galvanises the battle-brothers around them to reach new heights of righteous ferocity.

When resolving an attack made with a melee weapon by a friendly **BLACK TEMPLARS** unit within 6" of this Warlord, on an unmodified wound roll of 6 improve the Armour Penetration characteristic of that weapon for that attack by 1 (i.e. AP0 become AP-1, AP-1 becomes AP-2).

6 FRONT-LINE COMMANDER

Leading from the heart of the battle, the warlord pushes their brethren to ever more fervent acts of courage in the face of the enemy's guns.

When a friendly **BLACK TEMPLARS** unit within 6" of this Warlord Advances or makes a charge move, add 1 to the Advance roll or charge roll.

NAMED CHARACTERS

If one of the following characters is your Warlord, they must have the associated Warlord Trait shown below:

CHARACTER	WARLORD TRAIT
High Marshal Helbrecht	Front-line Commander
Chaplain Grimaldus	Epitome of Piety
The Emperor's Champion	Oathkeeper

STRATAGEMS

If your army is Battle-forged and includes any BLACK TEMPLARS Detachments (excluding Auxiliary Support Detachments), you have access to the Stratagems shown here.

1CP

ABHOR THE WITCH
Black Templars Stratagem
The Black Templars' zealous hatred of heretical sorcery steels their minds and bodies against psychic assaults.

Use this Stratagem in your opponent's Psychic phase, when an enemy PSYKER model manifests a psychic power within 24" of any BLACK TEMPLARS units from your army, after any Deny the Witch attempts have been made. Roll one D6; on a 4+ that psychic power is resisted.

1CP

CRUSADER RELICS
Black Templars Stratagem
The crusade ships of the Black Templars maintain vast armouries of blessed weapons and sacred artefacts.

Use this Stratagem before the battle. Select one BLACK TEMPLARS model from your army that has the word 'Sergeant' or 'Sword Brother' in their profile. That model can have one of the following Chapter Relics: Witchseeker Bolts, Sword of Judgement, Skull of the Cacodominus (pg 52). All of the Relics your army includes must be different and be given to different models.

1CP

DEVOUT PUSH
Black Templars Stratagem
The Black Templars hurl themselves into the enemy ranks.

Use this Stratagem at the start of the Fight phase. Select one BLACK TEMPLARS INFANTRY unit or one BLACK TEMPLARS BIKER unit from your army. Until the end of that phase, that unit can pile in and, when that unit consolidates, it can move up to 6" instead of 3".

2CP

TENACIOUS ASSAULT
Black Templars Stratagem
The Black Templars rarely permit their foes to retreat.

Use this Stratagem in the Movement phase, when an enemy INFANTRY unit that does not have the Flyer Battlefield Role and is within 1" of any BLACK TEMPLARS INFANTRY unit from your army is chosen to Fall Back. Roll one D6; on a 2+ that unit cannot Fall Back this turn.

1CP

THE EMPEROR'S WILL
Black Templars Stratagem
It is the divine command of the God-Emperor that the Black Templars bring ruin to Humanity's foes.

Use this Stratagem in your Movement phase, when a BLACK TEMPLARS INFANTRY unit from your army Advances. Until the end of this turn, models from that unit can still shoot with their Pistol weapons and the unit can still charge.

1CP

OATHS OF HONOUR
Black Templars Stratagem
As a Neophyte's apprenticeship ends, they fight all the harder to prove their Initiate's faith is not misplaced.

Use this Stratagem in the Fight phase. Select one BLACK TEMPLARS SCOUT unit from your army that made a charge move or was charged this turn. Until the end of that phase, when resolving an attack made with a melee weapon by a model in that unit, you can re-roll the wound roll.

1CP

VICIOUS RIPOSTE
Black Templars Stratagem
Every blow against a Black Templar is answered in kind.

Use this Stratagem in the Fight phase, when a BLACK TEMPLARS INFANTRY unit from your army is chosen as the target of an attack. Until the end of that phase, when resolving an attack made against that unit, on an unmodified save roll of 6 the attacking model's unit suffers 1 mortal wound after that unit has finished fighting.

1CP

SHOCK AND AWE
Black Templars Stratagem
The Black Templars strike with aggressive and overwhelming force, shattering their foes' will to fight.

Use this Stratagem in your Charge phase. Select one BLACK TEMPLARS INFANTRY unit from your army that disembarked from a LAND RAIDER CRUSADER this turn. Until the end of that turn, enemy units cannot fire Overwatch at the selected unit and, when resolving an attack made against that unit, subtract 1 from the hit roll.

CRUSADE RELICS

The holds of the Black Templars' crusade fleets are filled with innumerable prized relics and holy artefacts. Saved from destruction, they are preserved by a multitude of Chapter serfs, who meticulously maintain these sacred heirlooms in preparation for the day when they are ready to be carried to war in the Emperor's name.

If your army is led by a **BLACK TEMPLARS** Warlord, you can give one of the following Chapter Relics to a **BLACK TEMPLARS CHARACTER** model from your army instead of giving them a Relic from *Codex: Space Marines*. Named characters (such as Chaplain Grimaldus) and **VEHICLE** models cannot be given any of the following Relics.

Note that some Relics are weapons that replace one of the model's existing weapons. Where this is the case, you must, if you are using points values, still pay the cost of the weapon that is being replaced. Write down any Relics your models have on your army roster.

THE CRUSADER'S HELM

This imposing helm has been passed down to champions of the Black Templars for many centuries. Worked into its ancient vox-piece is the jawbone of Saint Sebatus the Ancient, a sanctified relic that emboldens the voice of the wearer so that his oratory soars above the clash of battle. The hearts of nearby battle-brothers are filled with zealous fire, and none can stand before their fury.

Add 3" to the range of a model with this Relic's aura abilities (to a maximum of 12"). In addition, at the start of your Movement phase, select one friendly **BLACK TEMPLARS** unit that has a Combat Doctrines ability (see *Codex: Space Marines*) and is within 6" of this model. Until the start of your next Movement phase, the Assault Doctrine becomes active for that unit, replacing the currently active combat doctrine.

WITCHSEEKER BOLTS

With the metal casings forged from the blades of fallen battle-brothers and blessed by the devout priests of the Ministorum, these bolt rounds have an unerring talent for finding their way to the heart of the witch.

Select one bolt weapon this model is equipped with (see *Codex: Space Marines*). When the bearer shoots with that weapon, you can choose for it to fire a witchseeker round. If you do, you can only make one attack with that weapon, but that attack can target a **PSYKER CHARACTER** unit even if it is not the closest enemy unit. When resolving an attack made with a witchseeker round against a **PSYKER** unit, if a hit is scored the target suffers D3 mortal wounds in addition to any other damage.

THE AURILLIAN SHROUD

Recovered from the shrine world of Aurilla after the opening of the Great Rift, this relic of devotion was once blessed by the holy form of Saint Agatine. Wreathed in an aura of coruscating light, the shroud is said to bring divine protection to all those who bask in its brilliance.

Once per battle, at the start of the battle round, a model with this Relic can unveil the Aurillian Shroud. Until the end of that battle round, models in friendly **BLACK TEMPLARS** units have a 4+ invulnerable save whilst their unit is within 3" of a model with this Relic.

ANCIENT BREVIARY

This humble prayer book once belonged to the first High Chaplain of the Black Templars. It contains his teachings on the divine, and his successors recite from its pages on the eve of battle. Every utterance from this tome carries immense weight for the battle-brothers of the Chapter.

CHAPLAIN model only. When a roll is made to determine if a litany recited by a model with this Relic is inspiring, you can roll two D6 and discard one of the results.

SKULL OF THE CACODOMINUS

A trophy taken from the period of time known only as the Howling, the skull of this wretched xenos creature still echoes with its monstrous, psychic death screams.

Once per battle, after a psychic power has been manifested by an enemy **PSYKER** model within 12" of a model with this Relic, roll one D6; on a 2+ that model suffers D3 mortal wounds after that psychic power has been resolved.

SWORD OF JUDGEMENT

The characteristic sigil of the Emperor's aquila adorns the cross guard of this revered blade, its keen edge having served many a Black Templar well over the millennia.

Model with a power sword or one master-crafted power sword only. This Relic replaces a power sword or master-crafted power sword and has the following profile:

WEAPON	RANGE	TYPE	S	AP	D
Sword of Judgement	Melee	Melee	+1	-3	3

POINTS VALUES

If you are playing a matched play game, or a game that uses a points limit, you can use the following lists to determine the total points cost of your army. Simply add together the points costs of all your models and the wargear they are equipped with to determine your army's total points value. The points costs for wargear can be found in *Codex: Space Marines*.

NAMED CHARACTERS

UNIT	MODELS PER UNIT	POINTS PER MODEL (Including wargear)
Chaplain Grimaldus	1	90
High Marshal Helbrecht	1	150
The Emperor's Champion	1	75

TROOPS

UNIT	MODELS PER UNIT	POINTS PER MODEL (Not including wargear)
Crusader Squad	5-20	13 (Neophyte is 11)

ELITES

UNIT	MODELS PER UNIT	POINTS PER MODEL (Including wargear)
Cenobyte Servitors	3	2

TACTICAL OBJECTIVES

The Black Templars epitomise the true ideals of the Imperial creed. Their martial prowess and dedication to their cause armour their souls against those who would seek to lay the Imperium low.

If your army is led by a **BLACK TEMPLARS** Warlord, these Tactical Objectives replace the Capture and Control Tactical Objectives (numbers 11-16) in the *Warhammer 40,000* rulebook. If a mission uses Tactical Objectives, players use the normal rules for using Tactical Objectives with the following exception: when a Black Templars player generates a Capture and Control objective (numbers 11-16), they instead generate the corresponding Black Templars Tactical Objective, as shown below. Other Tactical Objectives (numbers 21-66) are generated normally.

D66	TACTICAL OBJECTIVE
11	Decisive Action
12	Forthright Surety
13	Where It Hurts
14	Cast Down The Heathen
15	Aggressive Manoeuvre
16	Dictating The Flow

11 — DECISIVE ACTION

Strike with speed and determination in order to tip the battle in your favour.

Score 1 victory point for each enemy unit destroyed as a result of an attack made with a melee weapon by a **BLACK TEMPLARS** model from your army this turn (to a maximum of 3 victory points). Score an additional D3 victory points if the enemy Warlord was in one of those units.

Black Templars

12 — FORTHRIGHT SURETY

Only through personal sacrifice can one show true dedication to the Emperor.

Score 1 victory point if three or more **BLACK TEMPLARS** units from your army made a charge move or performed a Heroic Intervention this turn.

Black Templars

13 — WHERE IT HURTS

Prosecute the fight all the way to the heart of the enemy's power base.

Score 1 victory point if an enemy unit that started this turn wholly within its own deployment zone, and that suffered casualties as a result of attacks made by **BLACK TEMPLARS** models from your army this turn, was destroyed.

Black Templars

14 — CAST DOWN THE HEATHEN

The cankerous presence of the unclean must be scoured if one is to destroy their heretical influence.

Score 1 victory point if any enemy **CHARACTER** models were destroyed as a result of an attack made by a **BLACK TEMPLARS CHARACTER** model from your army this turn. If the enemy Warlord was destroyed as a result of an attack made by a **BLACK TEMPLARS CHARACTER** model from your army this turn, score D3 victory points instead.

Black Templars

15 — AGGRESSIVE MANOEUVRE

A conclusive strike is necessary if you are to prevent the enemy from establishing a foothold in the region.

Score 1 victory point if there are no **BLACK TEMPLARS** units from your army within your deployment zone at the end of your turn.

Black Templars

16 — DICTATING THE FLOW

The enemy seeks to delay the moment of contact to their own advantage, do not let this happen.

Score 1 victory point if any enemy units suffered any casualties as a result of attacks made by **BLACK TEMPLARS** models from your army that Advanced this turn. Score D3 victory points instead if three or more enemy units suffered any casualties as a result of attacks made by **BLACK TEMPLARS** models from your army that Advanced this turn.

Black Templars

BLACK TEMPLARS NAME GENERATOR

This section is a tool to help you forge a name for mighty warriors of your Chapter, to further build the background and personality of your army. If you wish to randomly generate a name for one of your Black Templars warriors, you can roll a D66 and consult the table below. To roll a D66, simply roll two D6, one after the other – the first represents tens, and the second represents digits, giving you a result between 11 and 66.

D66	NAME	D66	NAME
11	Ulrund	11	Zieger
12	Lyle	12	Arbrecht
13	Sagren	13	Kiergaard
14	Beus	14	Dranacht
15	Dietmar	15	Roellig
16	Magren	16	Narvecht
21	Kraus	21	Carlmagne
22	Magnor	22	Kraussar
23	Gresten	23	Gervaht
24	Breoc	24	Mordred
25	Ryker	25	Stabian
26	Otto	26	Kroeller
31	Arnulph	31	Emrik
32	Sebastian	32	Goraldus
33	Sapersperia qui	33	Bremon
34	Conrad	34	Sigenand
35	Leopus	35	Torismund
36	Vornus	36	Vorleii
41	Micael	41	Tovarus
42	Millian	42	Benedemnus
43	Niedrich	43	Lichtner
44	Alm	44	Vedrenn
45	Frederus	45	Siedrand
46	Charlus	46	Yorghast
51	Sedric	51	Velmnar
52	Beren	52	Bayard
53	Lothair	53	Zieter
54	Guy	54	Grosmund
55	Henraus	55	Havillan
56	Fedraus	56	Brichtus
61	Signar	61	Boremann
62	Hamlen	62	Richter
63	Avar	63	Ulbrecht
64	Diedrech	64	Zydwiege
65	Arnult	65	Illinecht
66	Raul	66	Paragund

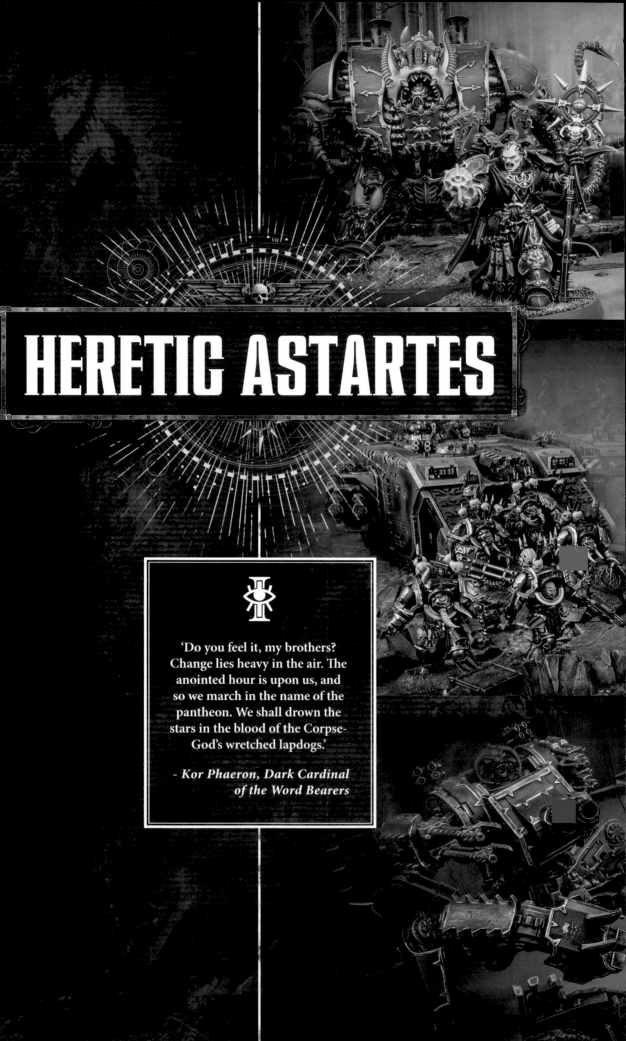

HERETIC ASTARTES

'Do you feel it, my brothers? Change lies heavy in the air. The anointed hour is upon us, and so we march in the name of the pantheon. We shall drown the stars in the blood of the Corpse-God's wretched lapdogs.'

- Kor Phaeron, Dark Cardinal of the Word Bearers

CHAMPIONS OF RUIN

The rules in this section supplement those found in *Codex: Chaos Space Marines* and can be used in any open play, narrative play or matched play game. They include new abilities for the Chaos Space Marines, new Artefacts of Chaos in the form of Daemon Weapons, and a swathe of new rules to further represent the infamous Legions of the Heretic Astartes.

ABILITIES

Chaos Space Marines **HERETIC ASTARTES** units (excluding **CULTISTS**) and **FALLEN** units gain the following additional abilities.

MALICIOUS VOLLEYS

To a Heretic Astartes the boltgun is far more than a weapon, it is an instrument of his anger and the bringer of death to his foes.

Instead of following the normal rules for Rapid Fire weapons, models in this unit firing Rapid Fire bolt weapons make double the number of attacks if any of the following apply:

- The firing model's target is within half the weapon's maximum range.
- The firing model is **INFANTRY** and every model in its unit remained stationary in your previous Movement phase.
- The firing model is a **TERMINATOR**, **BIKER** or **HELBRUTE**.

For the purposes of this ability, a Rapid Fire bolt weapon is any bolt weapon with the Rapid Fire type. A bolt weapon is any weapon whose profile includes the word 'bolt' (e.g. boltgun, bolt pistol, combi-bolter, Inferno boltgun). Rules that apply to bolt weapons also apply when firing the boltgun profile of combi-weapons and when firing Artefacts of Chaos that replaced a bolt weapon, (e.g. Spitespitter). The Talon of Horus is also a Rapid Fire bolt weapon.

HATEFUL ASSAULT

The Heretic Astartes are corrupted superhumans with ten thousand years of burning hatred. Few can withstand their hateful assault.

If this unit makes a charge move, is charged or performs a Heroic Intervention, add 1 to the Attacks characteristic of models in this unit until the end of the turn.

DAEMON WEAPONS

The selection of Relics presented on the following page represent a collection of Daemon Weapons. These are additional Artefacts of Chaos available to the Chaos Space Marines. If your army is led by a Chaos Space Marine Warlord, you can give one of them to a Chaos Space Marine **CHARACTER** model from your army, as you would an Artefact of Chaos.

Note that the weapons replace one of the character's existing weapons. You must, if you are playing a matched play game or are otherwise using points values, still pay the cost of the weapon that is being replaced. Write down any Artefacts of Chaos your characters have on your army roster.

> *'You fought bravely. You fought with skill and honour. Your comrades gave their lives to hold us at bay, and it was all for nothing. What has such blind faith earned you? Nothing but a torturous end at the edge of a ritual blade.'*
>
> - *Brother Duxartes of Crimson Slaughter*

UPDATED WEAPONRY

Since the publication of *Codex: Chaos Space Marines*, the characteristics profile of the demolisher cannon has changed. It now has the following profile:

WEAPON	RANGE	TYPE	S	AP	D
Demolisher cannon	24"	Heavy D6	10	-3	D6

DAEMON WEAPONS

If your army is led by a Chaos Space Marine Warlord, you can give one of these Artefacts of Chaos to a Chaos Space Marine CHARACTER model from your army, instead of the other Artefacts of Chaos presented in this publication or in *Codex: Chaos Space Marines*.

The Artefacts of Chaos listed here all have the following ability in addition to any others listed on their profile: 'Daemon Weapon: In the Fight phase, when this model is chosen to fight with for the first time that phase, roll one D6. On a 1, the model suffers 1 mortal wound and cannot use this weapon further that phase. On a 2+ the model can fight with the weapon as normal.'

Q'O'AK, THE BOUNDLESS

Q'o'ak drew Tzeentch's ire for ceaselessly tinkering with the plans of his Lords of Change, and thus was bound within this weapon to stop its tireless meddling. Yet when the weapon crosses blades with the bearer's enemies, a new victim falls foul of Q'o'ak temporal tampering. How Q'o'ak can traverse time whilst bound within its prison is unknown, yet for each soul Q'o'ak pulls from the path of fate, a fresh plume materialises from the weapon's hilt.

TZEENTCH model with power sword, hellforged sword or force sword only. This Relic replaces a power sword, hellforged sword or force sword and has the following profile:

WEAPON	RANGE	TYPE	S	AP	D
Q'o'ak	Melee	Melee	User	-3	D3

Abilities: When resolving an attack made with this weapon, invulnerable saves cannot be made.

THAA'RIS AND RHI'OL, THE RAPACIOUS TALONS

Thaa'ris and Rhi'ol were two rival Daemons who endlessly performed at the court of a great Daemon Prince. They drew their patron's displeasure when their competitive rivalry became the prime focus of their performances, neglecting the court and its lord. They were bound within two Daemon weapons, paired claws forever destined to dance at the behest of their bearer.

SLAANESH model with two lightning claws or two sets of malefic talons only. These Relics replace lightning claws or malefic talons and have the following profile:

WEAPON	RANGE	TYPE	S	AP	D
Thaa'ris and Rhi'ol	Melee	Melee	User	-2	2

Abilities: When resolving an attack made with this weapon, you can re-roll the wound roll. When rolling for this weapon's Daemon Weapon ability, on a 2+ you can make a number of additional attacks equal to the result with this weapon this phase.

ZAALL, THE WRATHFUL

Only Khorne's most incensed warriors can wield this blade. A Daemon of such unrestrained anger, Zaall was bound within to give a purpose to the Daemon's endless fury. Now the Daemon's anger ebbs and flows like a tide of gore synced to the wrath of its wielder.

KHORNE model with power sword or hellforged sword only. This Relic replaces a power sword or hellforged sword and has the following profile:

WEAPON	RANGE	TYPE	S	AP	D
Zaall	Melee	Melee	User	-5	2

Abilities: When rolling for this weapon's Daemon Weapon ability, on a 2+ add a number to this weapon's Strength characteristic equal to the result until the end of this phase.

G'HOLL'AX, FIST OF DECAY

The very essence of pestilence exudes from the fingertips of this malign artefact. Said to have been gifted by the Lord of Decay himself, the mortal that bears this symbolic weapon is a herald of contagion and a physical example that none can resist the inescapable grip of decay.

NURGLE model with power fist only. This Relic replaces a power fist and has the following profile:

WEAPON	RANGE	TYPE	S	AP	D
G'holl'ax	Melee	Melee	x2	-3	3

Abilities: When resolving an attack made with this weapon, subtract 1 from the hit roll, and an unmodified wound roll of 2+ is always successful.

UL'O'CCA, THE BLACK AXE

This axe was found on a Daemon world resting in a cavern marked with diabolical wards. Thousands of corpses lay at its feet, sacrificial offerings from an unknown warden to appease its hunger. One brave soul now seeks to feed the Daemon by other means.

Model with power axe, force axe or daemonic axe only. This Relic replaces a power axe, force axe or daemonic axe and has the following profile:

WEAPON	RANGE	TYPE	S	AP	D
Ul'o'cca	Melee	Melee	User	0	1

Abilities: When resolving an attack made with this weapon, an unmodified wound roll of 4+ inflicts 1 mortal wound on the target in addition to any other damage.

WORD BEARERS

In this section you'll find rules for Battle-forged armies that include WORD BEARERS Detachments – that is, any Detachment that includes only WORD BEARERS units. These include a series of Warlord Traits, Stratagems, Artefacts of Chaos and Tactical Objectives. Together, these reflect the character and fighting style of the Word Bearers in your games of Warhammer 40,000.

INTRODUCTION

The rules presented in this section are intended to be used in addition to those presented in *Codex: Chaos Space Marines* if you have chosen to take any WORD BEARERS Detachments. A WORD BEARERS Detachment is still treated as a Chaos Space Marine Detachment for the purposes of the Stratagems, Artefacts of Chaos and Warlord Traits presented in *Codex: Chaos Space Marines*. The following additional rules apply.

WARLORD TRAITS

If a WORD BEARERS CHARACTER model is your Warlord, you can use the Warlord Traits table on the page opposite instead of those found in other publications to determine what Warlord Trait they have. These allow you to tailor your Warlord to display the typical traits of the leaders of the Legion.

STRATAGEMS

If your army is Battle-forged and includes any WORD BEARERS Detachments, the Stratagems on page 62 can be used in addition to those presented in *Codex: Chaos Space Marines* to reflect the fighting style of the Legion.

ARTEFACTS OF THE WORD BEARERS

Page 63 presents a collection of infamous Relics of the Legion. If your army is led by a Chaos Space Marine Warlord, you can give one of these Artefacts of Chaos to a WORD BEARERS CHARACTER model from your army, instead of those

found elsewhere in this publication and in other publications.

Note that some weapons replace one of the character's existing weapons. Where this is the case you must, if you are playing a matched play game or are otherwise using points values, still pay the cost of the weapon that is being replaced. Write down any Artefacts of Chaos your models have on your army roster.

TACTICAL OBJECTIVES

Page 64 provides new Tactical Objectives for use in Maelstrom of War missions to represent the strategies and tactics of the Legion on the battlefield.

NAME GENERATOR

On page 65 you will find a useful tool to help you forge a name for mighty warriors of your Legion, further building the background and personality of your army.

> 'Cast down the idols! Destroy the temples! Slay the priests! Show these fools that they worship nothing more than a rotting corpse!'
>
> - Dark Apostle Harzhan of the Word Bearers

WORD BEARERS WARLORD TRAITS

If a WORD BEARERS CHARACTER model is your Warlord, you can use the Word Bearers Warlord Traits table below to determine what Warlord Trait they have. You can either roll one D6 on the table below to randomly generate a Warlord Trait, or you can select the one that best suits your Warlord's preferred style of waging war.

D6 WARLORD TRAIT

1 THE VOICE OF LORGAR

This warlord speaks with the authority of his Primarch; when he commands, others follow without question or hesitation.

Add 3" to the range of this Warlord's aura abilities (e.g. Lord of Chaos).

2 EXALTED POSSESSION

This warlord shares his flesh with a powerful Daemon. Physically stronger and faster than mere mortals, he venerates the pantheon with this union.

This Warlord gains the POSSESSED and DAEMON keywords (if they don't already have them). Add 1 to the Strength and Attacks characteristics of this Warlord, and add 1" to this Warlord's Move characteristic.

3 DAEMONIC WHISPERS

Blessings from the empyrean guide this warlord and his followers.

If your army is Battle-forged, roll one D3 before the battle begins; you gain a number of additional Command Points equal to the result. Once per battle, if this Warlord is on the battlefield, you can re-roll a single hit roll, wound roll, damage roll or saving throw.

4 MASTER OF THE UNION

This warlord leads their daemonic brethren with fearsome influence, drawing forth the unholy emotions of the corrupted.

Add 1 to the Attacks characteristic of models in friendly WORD BEARERS DAEMON units whilst their unit is within 6" of this Warlord.

5 DIABOLIST

This warlord etches diabolical incantations into their armour and skin to channel the protection of the warp.

When this Warlord would lose a wound, roll one D6, adding 3 to the result if that wound would be lost as the result of a mortal wound; on a 6+ that wound is not lost.

6 SACRILEGIOUS REGENERATION

Giving up one's soul and purpose to the Dark Gods has garnered their favour. The very energy of the immaterium now seeps through this warlord's veins, healing afflictions of the material realm.

Add 1 to this Warlord's Wounds characteristic. At the start of your turn, this Warlord regains up to D3 lost wounds.

WORD BEARERS STRATAGEMS

If your army is Battle-forged and includes any WORD BEARERS Detachments (excluding Auxiliary Support Detachments), you have access to the Stratagems shown here.

DARK PACT
1CP

Word Bearers Stratagem

The Word Bearers are experts at drawing the twisted minions of the Dark Gods into realspace, using profane rituals and gruesome sacrifices.

Use this Stratagem at the end of your Movement phase, when a **WORD BEARERS CHARACTER** model from your army attempts to summon a unit of **DAEMONS** to the battlefield using a Daemonic Ritual. When making the summoning roll for that attempt, you can re-roll the dice and this **CHARACTER** model will not suffer any mortal wounds for rolling doubles or triples.

MALEVOLENT COVENANT
1CP

Word Bearers Stratagem

The powers of the warp will provide for the faithful, but a price must always be paid.

Use this Stratagem in your Psychic phase, after a **WORD BEARERS PSYKER** unit from your army fails a Psychic test. The power is automatically manifested by that **PSYKER** unit at the minimum required warp charge value and without a double having been rolled, and cannot be resisted by a Deny the Witch attempt. After resolving the effects of the psychic power, that **PSYKER** unit suffers 1 mortal wound.

APOSTLE OF THE DARK COUNCIL
1CP

Word Bearers Stratagem

The ruling leaders of the Word Bearers guide their Legion on matters of faith as much as war.

Use this Stratagem before the battle. Select one **WORD BEARERS PRIEST** model from your army. That model gains the following ability: 'Dark Council: This model knows one additional prayer from the Prayers to the Dark Gods (see *Codex: Chaos Space Marines*), and can chant one additional prayer at the start of the battle round.' You can only use this Stratagem once per battle.

CURSED DESPOILERS
2CP

Word Bearers Stratagem

Every stone is an affront to the gods that must be toppled.

Use this Stratagem after deployment but before the first battle round begins, if a **WORD BEARERS** unit from your army is on the battlefield. Select one terrain feature (other than a Fortification). Units entirely on or within that terrain feature do not gain the benefit of cover to their saving throws.

REVERED HOSTS
1CP

Word Bearers Stratagem

There is no greater way to venerate Chaos than to bond mortal with Daemon.

Use this Stratagem in the Fight phase, when a **WORD BEARERS POSSESSED** unit or **WORD BEARERS GREATER POSSESSED** unit from your army is chosen to fight with. Until the end of the phase, add 1 to the Damage characteristic of melee weapons models in that unit are equipped with.

HEXAGRAMMATIC WARD
1CP

Word Bearers Stratagem

Diabolical wards of protection can turn aside the enemy's blows.

Use this Stratagem in any phase, after making a saving throw for a **WORD BEARERS CHARACTER** model from your army. Treat the result of that saving throw as 6. Each **WORD BEARERS CHARACTER** model from your army can only be the target of this Stratagem once per battle.

VENGEANCE FOR MONARCHIA
1CP

Word Bearers Stratagem

Never will the outrage on beloved Monarchia be forgiven.

Use this Stratagem in the Fight phase, when a **WORD BEARERS** unit from your army is chosen to fight with. Until the end of that phase, when resolving an attack made with a melee weapon by a model in that unit against an **ULTRAMARINES** unit, you can re-roll the hit roll and you can re-roll the wound roll.

ARTEFACTS OF THE WORD BEARERS

If your army is led by a Chaos Space Marine Warlord, you can give one of these Artefacts of Chaos to a WORD BEARERS CHARACTER model from your army, instead of other Artefacts of Chaos presented elsewhere.

CROWN OF THE BLASPHEMER

Adorned with the finger bones of defiant men and anointed with the blood of unbelievers, the Crown of the Blasphemer attracts the attention of Warp entities to the wearer. Upon the battlefield, powered blades are turned away by invisible hands, thunderous volleys of bullets are snatched into the aether at the last moment, and enemy warriors find their minds assailed with visions of a galaxy in flames.

Improve the invulnerable save of a model with this Relic by 1, to a maximum of 3+. Subtract 1 from the Leadership characteristic of models in enemy units whilst their unit is within 6" of this model.

BALEFUL ICON

This icon bears an eight-pointed star so saturated in the blood of loyalists that it is forever stained with the taint of treachery. Those who wish the bearer harm find their certainty sapped away by the mere proximity of this blasphemous standard. The Word Bearers that carry it feel its toxic aura much as a sun worshipper feels the kiss of a summer day upon his skin. Those who do not worship the Dark Gods instead find their skin crawling and their muscles shuddering in revulsion. Even Adeptus Astartes are drained of their righteous anger in its presence.

When a charge roll is made for a charge declared against any friendly WORD BEARERS units within 6" of a model with this Relic, subtract 2 from the result.

BOOK OF THE REVILER

None can truly say what knowledge the Book of the Reviler contains. One glimpse at its pages is an affront to the senses, a sickening assault on one's sanity at the barbarous truths the tome contains. Those with the fortitude to read the lines of this heinous opus manifest mutated boons of Chaos for their efforts.

Model that is not a DAEMON only. Before the battle, a model with this Relic can read from the Book of the Reviler. If it does, randomly generate two Chaos Boons for that model from the table found in the Chaos Boon Stratagem (see *Codex: Chaos Space Marines*), re-rolling Spawndom and Daemonhood and duplicate results. Note that doing so does not cost any Command Points, and an enemy CHARACTER, VEHICLE or MONSTER model does not have to have been destroyed.

THE MALEFIC TOME

This unholy tome has been stitched together from the flayed skins of a dozen mortal psykers. Each leathery page still bears the hairs and birthmarks of the book's unwilling donors, their horror emanating from every inch of stolen skin. The book's leaves are inscribed with true names, hexagrammatic diagrams and daemonic hierarchies that offer the bearer abominable insights into the powers of the Warp.

PSYKER model only. A model with this Relic knows one additional psychic power from their chosen discipline. When a Psychic test is taken for a model with this Relic, add 1 to the total.

ASHEN AXE

The Ashen Axe dates back to the Great Crusade, a vicious chainaxe that was oft used on the citizens of worlds that rejected compliance. As the Legion descended into darkness, Daemons of the Warp were drawn in, feeding off the anguish and misery that its chained blades created. The Ashen Axe has become a malefic nexus for the creatures of the immaterium. Enemies of the Word Bearers find themselves unable to flee from the axe's blows, as claws and talons grasp at their limbs and root them to the spot. In truth, their minds are assailed by the entities of the aether, circling impatiently for the soul feast the Ashen Axe will deliver.

Model with chainaxe only. This Relic replaces a chainaxe and has the following profile:

WEAPON	RANGE	TYPE	S	AP	D
Ashen Axe	Melee	Melee	+1	-2	D3

Abilities: Enemy units within 1" of a model with this Relic cannot Fall Back unless they have the VEHICLE or TITANIC keyword, or have a minimum Move characteristic.

EPISTLE OF LORGAR

One hallowed artefact above all is an epistle from the Book of Lorgar. When a priest reads from its pages, the very air turns metallic and the words summon dark blessings from the immaterium. All those who accept the words into their soul are imbued with its energy.

PRIEST model only. When a model with this Relic chants a prayer, you can re-roll the dice to determine if that prayer is heard. Add 1 to the Leadership characteristic of models in friendly WORD BEARERS units whilst their unit is within 6" of this model.

WORD BEARERS TACTICAL OBJECTIVES

These Tactical Objectives are for use in Maelstrom of War missions to represent the strategies and tactics of the Legion on the battlefield.

If your army is led by a **WORD BEARERS** Warlord, these Tactical Objectives replace the Capture and Control Tactical Objectives (numbers 11-16) in the *Warhammer 40,000* rulebook. If a mission uses Tactical Objectives, players use the normal rules for using Tactical Objectives with the following exception: when a Word Bearers player generates a Capture and Control objective (numbers 11-16), they instead generate the corresponding Word Bearers Tactical Objective, as shown below. Other Tactical Objectives (numbers 21-66) are generated normally.

D66	TACTICAL OBJECTIVE
11	Feed the Daemon
12	Exalt the Dark Gods
13	Grisly Sacrifice
14	Consecrated Ground
15	Slay False Prophets
16	Cast Down False Idols

11 — FEED THE DAEMON

Your unholy allies must feed upon the flesh of the enemy and, in doing so, devour their souls.

Score 1 victory point if an enemy unit was destroyed as a result of an attack made with a melee weapon by a **DAEMON** model from your army this turn.

Word Bearers

12 — EXALT THE DARK GODS

Venerate the empyrean through deed and action.

Score 1 victory point if any prayers chanted by **WORD BEARERS** models from your army were heard this turn, or any **WORD BEARERS** model from your army manifested any psychic powers this turn.

Word Bearers

13 — GRISLY SACRIFICE

Ritualistic sacrifice is a worthy price to pay for the powers of the immaterium.

Score 1 victory point for each **WORD BEARERS** unit from your army that was destroyed in the Fight phase of this turn and 1 victory point for each enemy unit that was destroyed as the result of an attack made by a **WORD BEARERS** model from your army in the Fight phase of this turn, to a maximum of 6 victory points.

Word Bearers

14 — CONSECRATED GROUND

Let us offer up these lands to the gods, and from this hallowed ground call forth the power of Chaos.

Score 1 victory point if you control an objective marker with any **WORD BEARERS CHARACTER** unit from your army at the end of your turn.

Word Bearers

15 — SLAY FALSE PROPHETS

Prove the terrible might of those dedicated to Chaos by spilling the blood of rival champions and icons.

Score D3 victory points if any enemy units with the HQ or Lord of War Battlefield Role were destroyed this turn.

Word Bearers

16 — CAST DOWN FALSE IDOLS

The Word Bearers take cruel enjoyment in defiling the havens of their enemies.

Score 1 victory point if you have at least one **WORD BEARERS** unit from your army wholly within the enemy's deployment zone at the end of your turn. If you have at least one **WORD BEARERS** unit from your army wholly within the enemy's deployment zone and controlling an objective marker at the end of your turn, score D3 victory points instead.

Word Bearers

WORD BEARERS NAME GENERATOR

This section is a tool to help you forge a name for mighty warriors of your Legion, to further build the background and personality of your army. If you wish to randomly generate a name for one of your Word Bearers warriors, you can roll a D66 and consult the table below. To roll a D66, simply roll two D6, one after the other – the first represents tens, and the second represents digits, giving you a result between 11 and 66.

D66	FIRST NAME		D66	LAST NAME
11	Atresh		11	Kartho
12	Sadu		12	Layak
13	Borek		13	Gallek
14	Nar		14	Arthustra
15	Argel		15	Talgron
16	Tarem		16	Ranasar
21	Kor		21	Peroth
22	Baruk		22	Mairon
23	Noros		23	Grelloth
24	Baleros		24	Merenkar
25	Torek		25	Sethilon
26	Darad		26	Vhanalis
31	Kurtha		31	Khedimar
32	Sor		32	Sa'quath
33	Bathusa		33	Xesugal
34	Iarto		34	Caeroth
35	Koros		35	Demnos
36	Ban		36	Iagath
41	Sorot		41	Drennulan
42	Xaphen		42	Kayadim
43	Daroth		43	Saeperath
44	Vhol		44	Gorlem
45	Bara		45	Vondar
46	Peros		46	Quroth
51	Aspin		51	Okoleth
52	Verok		52	Vhandrax
53	Qarad		53	Tchure
54	Kemak		54	Derenoth
55	Arthul		55	Khoura
56	Thulo		56	Gharax
61	Jadath		61	Iennos
62	Sumon		62	Jadimas
63	Dashul		63	Ennat
64	Halam		64	Bol
65	Cenat		65	Ennar
66	Kalim		66	Tal

NIGHT LORDS

In this section you'll find rules for Battle-forged armies that include NIGHT LORDS Detachments – that is, any Detachment that includes only NIGHT LORDS units. These include a series of Warlord Traits, Stratagems, Artefacts of Chaos and Tactical Objectives. Together, these reflect the character and fighting style of the Night Lords in your games of Warhammer 40,000.

INTRODUCTION

The rules presented in this section are intended to be used in addition to those presented in *Codex: Chaos Space Marines* if you have chosen to take any **NIGHT LORDS** Detachments. A **NIGHT LORDS** Detachment is still treated as a Chaos Space Marine Detachment for the purposes of the Stratagems, Artefacts of Chaos and Warlord Traits presented in *Codex: Chaos Space Marines*. The following additional rules apply.

WARLORD TRAITS

If a **NIGHT LORDS CHARACTER** model is your Warlord, you can use the Warlord Traits table on the page opposite instead of those found in other publications to determine what Warlord Trait they have. These allow you to tailor your Warlord to display the typical traits of the leaders of the Legion.

STRATAGEMS

If your army is Battle-forged and includes any **NIGHT LORDS** Detachments, the Stratagems on page 68 can be used in addition to those presented in *Codex: Chaos Space Marines* to reflect the fighting style of the Legion.

ARTEFACTS OF THE NIGHT LORDS

Page 69 presents a collection of infamous Relics of the Legion. If your army is led by a Chaos Space Marine Warlord, you can give one of these Artefacts of Chaos to a **NIGHT LORDS CHARACTER** model from your army, instead of those found elsewhere in this publication and in other publications.

Note that some weapons replace one of the character's existing weapons. Where this is the case, you must, if you are playing a matched play game or are otherwise using points values, still pay the cost of the weapon that is being replaced. Write down any Artefacts of Chaos your models have on your army roster.

TACTICAL OBJECTIVES

Page 70 provides new Tactical Objectives for use in Maelstrom of War missions to represent the strategies and tactics of the Legion on the battlefield.

NAME GENERATOR

On page 71 you will find a useful tool to help you forge a name for mighty warriors of your Legion, further building the background and personality of your army.

'The light of the False Emperor is gone. Darkness descends. For we who were born of the night, we who stalk in midnight clad, the Great Haunting begins. Let screams fill the air, terror run rampant and skins fill the pits.'

- Lord Yharas Kine

NIGHT LORDS WARLORD TRAITS

If a NIGHT LORDS CHARACTER model is your Warlord, you can use the Night Lords Warlord Traits table below to determine what Warlord Trait they have. You can either roll one D6 on the table below to randomly generate a Warlord Trait, or you can select the one that best suits your Warlord's preferred style of waging war.

D6 WARLORD TRAIT

1 NIGHT HAUNTER'S CURSE

Some Night Lords warlords share the same curse of foresight that plagued their Primarch.

Once per battle round, you can re-roll a single hit roll, wound roll, damage roll, Advance roll, charge roll or saving throw made for this Warlord.

2 ONE PIECE AT A TIME

This warlord prefers to toy with his prey, striking hard and fast, then vanishing once more, his injured and helpless victims completely at his mercy.

This Warlord can charge in a turn in which they Fell Back. When resolving an attack made with a melee weapon against this Warlord, subtract 1 from the hit roll.

3 MURDEROUS REPUTATION

Even amongst a breed of murderers, this warlord has gained a notorious reputation for his mastery of the killing art.

When resolving an attack made by this Warlord, an unmodified hit roll of 6 inflicts 1 mortal wound on the target in addition to any other damage.

4 KILLING FURY

This warlord launches himself into the heart of enemy lines to slake his thirst for butchery.

Add D3 to the Attacks characteristic of this Warlord in a turn in which they made a charge move, were charged or performed a Heroic Intervention. These additional attacks last until the end of the Fight phase.

5 ONE WITH THE SHADOWS

So skilled at blending into darkness is this warlord, that it is difficult to discern where his corporeal form ends and the shadows begin.

When resolving an attack made against this Warlord whilst they are entirely on or within a terrain feature, add 1 to the saving throw (excluding invulnerable saving throws). Whilst this Warlord is entirely on or within a terrain feature, improve its invulnerable save by 1, to a maximum of 3+ (e.g. a 4+ invulnerable save becomes 3+).

6 DIRTY FIGHTER

To this warlord, the very notion of fighting fair is alien. He will gang up with his brothers to lay low the enemy.

Whilst there are more friendly models within 3" of this Warlord than enemy models, when resolving an attack made with a melee weapon by this Warlord, add 1 to the wound roll.

'Honour is nothing more than the last refuge of fools. Look upon the butchered corpses of your comrades and tell me again what your precious honour is worth.'

- Brother Tavor Syke of the Whispering Shadow

NIGHT LORDS STRATAGEMS

If your army is Battle-forged and includes any NIGHT LORDS Detachments (excluding Auxiliary Support Detachments), you have access to the Stratagems shown here.

IN MIDNIGHT CLAD
1CP

Night Lords Stratagem

Having fought countless campaigns of terror in complete darkness, the Night Lords know how to make an ally of the shadows.

Use this Stratagem in your opponent's Shooting phase, when a NIGHT LORDS INFANTRY unit from your army is targeted by a shooting attack. Until the end of that phase, when resolving an attack against that unit, subtract 1 from the hit roll.

WE HAVE COME FOR YOU
1CP

Night Lords Stratagem

When the Night Lords descend, there is no mercy.

Use this Stratagem at the start of your opponent's Movement phase. Select one NIGHT LORDS unit from your army that is not a VEHICLE. Until the start of your next turn, enemy units within 1" of that unit cannot Fall Back unless they have the VEHICLE or TITANIC keyword, or have a minimum Move characteristic.

VOX SCREAM
2CP

Night Lords Stratagem

Hideous screams of an aggressive techno-virus infiltrate the communication systems of the target, temporarily rendering it incapable of command.

Use this Stratagem at the end of your Movement phase. Select one enemy unit within 18" of any NIGHT LORDS units from your army. Until the start of your next Movement phase, enemy units cannot be affected by any of the selected unit's aura abilities.

FROM THE NIGHT
1CP

Night Lords Stratagem

The sons of Nostramo strike from the dark.

Use this Stratagem at the start of your Charge phase. Select one NIGHT LORDS INFANTRY unit from your army that is entirely on or within a terrain feature. Until the end of the turn, when a charge roll is made for that unit, add 2 to the result, and when resolving an attack made with a melee weapon by a model in that unit, add 1 to the hit roll.

PREY ON THE WEAK
1CP

Night Lords Stratagem

Striking at the will of their victims, the meek of mind are the quarry of the VIII Legion.

Use this Stratagem in your Shooting phase or the Fight phase, when a NIGHT LORDS unit from your army is chosen to shoot or fight with. Until the end of that phase, when resolving an attack made by a model in that unit against an enemy unit whose models have a lower Leadership characteristic than the attacking model, add 1 to the hit roll.

RAPTOR STRIKE
1CP

Night Lords Stratagem

Raptor cults circle above their prey, then descend when their victims are otherwise afflicted.

Use this Stratagem in your Charge phase, before making a charge roll for a NIGHT LORDS JUMP PACK unit from your army that was set up on the battlefield as reinforcements this turn. Roll 3D6 for that charge roll instead of 2D6.

HIT AND RUN
1CP

Night Lords Stratagem

There is no honourable fight, only darting strikes, feigned retreats and all manner of dirty tactics to win the battle.

Use this Stratagem at the start of your Charge phase. Select one NIGHT LORDS unit from your army. That unit can charge even if it Fell Back this turn.

FLAY THEM ALIVE
1CP

Night Lords Stratagem

Death does not always follow defeat.

Use this Stratagem in the Fight phase, when an enemy unit is destroyed as a result of an attack made by a NIGHT LORDS model from your army. Until the end of the turn, when a Morale test is taken for an enemy unit within 12" of that NIGHT LORDS unit, your opponent must roll one additional D6 and you can choose one of those dice to be discarded.

ARTEFACTS OF THE NIGHT LORDS

If your army is led by a Chaos Space Marine Warlord, you can give one of these Artefacts of Chaos to a NIGHT LORDS CHARACTER from your army, instead of other Artefacts of Chaos presented elsewhere.

FLAYER

When the Legion's frightful tendencies came to the fore, the Flayer was the tool that carved the skin to be hung in the Night Haunter's throne room. The foulest of deeds were done with this blade, and its reputation grew within the VIII as a relic of dread. Only the most malevolent Legionnaires can bear its heinous lineage.

Model with power sword only. This Relic replaces a power sword and has the following profile:

WEAPON	RANGE	TYPE	S	AP	D
Flayer	Melee	Melee	+1	-3	2

Abilities: Each model destroyed by an attack with this weapon counts as two for the purposes of Morale tests.

STORMBOLT PLATE

This artificer armour was fashioned from a strange metal smelted in the darkest pits of long dead Nostramo. It is not the war-plate's incredible durability, however, that has made it so prized amongst the Night Lords. It is wreathed in a cloying darkness, an unnatural skein of midnight that perpetually shrouds the wearer. So it is that a warrior with the Stormbolt Plate pounces on their prey from the shadows.

INFANTRY model only. A model with this Relic has a Save characteristic of 2+. In addition, a model with this Relic always counts as being in cover, even while it is not entirely on or within a terrain feature.

VOX DAEMONICUS

Emanating from the ornate winged helm in which it makes its home, a living susurrus haunts the airwaves, spreading lies and falsehoods across the vox networks of the Night Lords' enemies. The chill whispers of the Vox Daemonicus have unmanned brave commanders and undermined masterful strategies; many a best-laid plan has been torn to shreds by its baleful curse.

INFANTRY model only. Whilst an enemy unit is within 6" of a model with this Relic, reduce the range of that unit's aura abilities to 1". In addition, enemy units that are set up on the battlefield as reinforcements cannot be set up within 12" of a model with this Relic.

TALONS OF THE NIGHT TERROR

Worn over a pair of boots, these talons give the wielder the appearance of some eldritch raptor-beast that has evolved to better disembowel prey. Should one sporting these bladed accoutrements descend feet first into the ranks of his quarry, the talons will eviscerate all those too slow to evade them. A heartbeat later, the crushing weight of the Chaos Space Marine wearer will be brought to bear with sickening, spine breaking impact.

Model that can FLY only. This Relic has the following profile:

WEAPON	RANGE	TYPE	S	AP	D
Talons of the Night Terror	Melee	Melee	+1	-1	1

Abilities: When a model with this Relic fights, it makes D3 additional attacks with this weapon, or D6 additional attacks with this weapon if it made a charge move or performed a Heroic Intervention this turn.

SCOURGING CHAINS

The Scourging Chains once jangled from the rafters of the Primarch's throne room. Many a soul judged guilty by the Night Haunter has been hanged from their jagged spikes. As the wearer flies towards his victims, these spiked chains appear taut as corded tendons, loosening and looping before impact. By lashing out and making sharp contact, captured prey are helpless to avoid the killing blow.

Improve the Armour Penetration characteristic of melee weapons a model with this Relic is equipped with by 1 (e.g. AP 0 becomes AP -1). Subtract 1 from the Attacks characteristic (to a minimum of 1) of enemy models whilst they are within 1" of a model with this Relic.

MISERY OF THE MEEK

This elixir is crafted by one of the Legion's few remaining apothecaries. He will hunt Legion slaves, scraping a life of meagre existence in the dark recesses of Night Lords vessels, and distil the fear and suffering of these unfortunate victims. Vials are then sold for supplies, passage and power. When a son of Nostramo indulges in the sickening contents, they are imbued with new energy.

Once per battle, at the start of your Movement phase, a model with this Relic can drink from the Misery of Meek. That model immediately regains up to D6 lost wounds, and until the start of your next turn, add D3 to that model's Attacks characteristic.

NIGHT LORDS TACTICAL OBJECTIVES

These Tactical Objectives are for use in Maelstrom of War missions to represent the strategies and tactics of the Legion on the battlefield.

If your army is led by a **NIGHT LORDS** Warlord, these Tactical Objectives replace the Capture and Control Tactical Objectives (numbers 11-16) in the *Warhammer 40,000* rulebook. If a mission uses Tactical Objectives, players use the normal rules for using Tactical Objectives with the following exception: when a Night Lords player generates a Capture and Control objective (numbers 11-16), they instead generate the corresponding Night Lords Tactical Objective, as shown below. Other Tactical Objectives (numbers 21-66) are generated normally.

D66	TACTICAL OBJECTIVE
11	Strike as if from Nowhere
12	Murder on the Mind
13	Charnel House
14	Bringers of Terror
15	Hunter, Prey
16	Genocidal Tendencies

11 — STRIKE AS IF FROM NOWHERE

A favoured strategy of the Night Lords is to launch sudden and hard-hitting strikes, be they from the skies, concealed positions or the enemy's flanks.

Score 1 victory point if an enemy unit was destroyed this turn as the result of an attack made by a **NIGHT LORDS** model from your army whose unit was either entirely on or within a terrain feature or arrived as reinforcements this turn.

Night Lords

12 — MURDER ON THE MIND

The Night Lords never pass up an opportunity for a gory display of brutality.

Score 1 victory point if an enemy unit was destroyed in the Fight phase of this turn as a result of an attack made by a **NIGHT LORDS** model from your army that made a charge move or performed a Heroic Intervention this turn.

Night Lords

13 — CHARNEL HOUSE

When the Night Lords capture key locations they turn them into charnel houses, as a grisly reminder to all that the VIII are the bringers of horror.

Score D3 victory points if you control an objective marker with any **NIGHT LORDS** units from your army at the end of your turn and that objective marker was controlled by your opponent at the start of your turn.

Night Lords

14 — BRINGERS OF TERROR

Honouring the ways of their Primarch's reign of terror on ancient Nostramo, the Night Lords use fear as a weapon as much as bolter and blade.

Score 1 victory point for each enemy unit that failed a Morale test this turn (or D3 victory points if the enemy unit was destroyed as a result of the failed Morale test), to a maximum of 6 victory points.

Night Lords

15 — HUNTER, PREY

The Night Lords prey upon the weakling champions of lesser foes with cruel pleasure.

Score D3 victory points if an enemy **CHARACTER** model was destroyed as the result of an attack made by a **NIGHT LORDS** model from your army this turn.

Night Lords

16 — GENOCIDAL TENDENCIES

The Night Lords can often be seen giving in to their baser instincts and hurling themselves at the foe indiscriminately.

Score 1 victory point if two or more **NIGHT LORDS** units from your army made a charge move this turn.

Night Lords

NIGHT LORDS NAME GENERATOR

This section is a tool to help you forge a name for mighty warriors of your Legion, to further build the background and personality of your army. If you wish to randomly generate a name for one of your Night Lords warriors, you can roll a D66 and consult the table below. To roll a D66, simply roll two D6, one after the other – the first represents tens, and the second represents digits, giving you a result between 11 and 66.

D66	NAME		D66	NAME
11	Thavor		11	Morgaris
12	Talos		12	Nosferrus
13	Daras		13	Khade
14	Navir		14	Varclav
15	Jago		15	Shadom
16	Zsaros		16	the Flayer
21	Kharros		21	Reeve
22	Gudel		22	Khravor
23	Naravesh		23	Souleater
24	Yudesh		24	the Feared
25	Ruvihr		25	Carrow
26	Vastiani		26	Virrikor
31	Ioden		31	Krouss
32	Ravkos		32	Sahaal
33	Sarran		33	of the Ceaseless Torment
34	Malithos		34	Narvirok
35	Koor		35	Zharost
36	Cel		36	Nightblade
41	Lavir		41	Vakkaris
42	Resk		42	Taravakh
43	Ullim		43	Envorros
44	Sanad		44	Terask
45	Otho		45	Mercygiver
46	Tovac		46	Reskian
51	Mirac		51	Crutian
52	Drachos		52	the Agoniser
53	Saveth		53	Balicor
54	Myros		54	Naevian
55	Vandred		55	Sarimund
56	Keth		56	of the Midnight Claw
61	Garras		61	Udreth
62	Qoros		62	Kavatar
63	Reskil		63	Sevataris
64	Amathus		64	Rudesk
65	Volis		65	Vharaun
66	Raddesk		66	Baraski

ALPHA LEGION

In this section you'll find rules for Battle-forged armies that include ALPHA LEGION Detachments – that is, any Detachment that includes only ALPHA LEGION units. These include a series of Warlord Traits, Stratagems, Artefacts of Chaos and Tactical Objectives. Together, these reflect the character and fighting style of the Alpha Legion in your games of Warhammer 40,000.

INTRODUCTION

The rules presented in this section are intended to be used in addition to those presented in *Codex: Chaos Space Marines* if you have chosen to take any ALPHA LEGION Detachments. An ALPHA LEGION Detachment is still treated as a Chaos Space Marine Detachment for the purposes of the Stratagems, Artefacts of Chaos and Warlord Traits presented in *Codex: Chaos Space Marines*. The following additional rules apply:

WARLORD TRAITS

If an ALPHA LEGION CHARACTER model is your Warlord, you can use the Warlord Traits table on the page opposite instead of those found in other publications to determine what Warlord Trait they have. These allow you to tailor your Warlord to display the typical traits of the leaders of the Legion.

STRATAGEMS

If your army is Battle-forged and includes any ALPHA LEGION Detachments, the Stratagems on page 74 can be used in addition to those presented in *Codex: Chaos Space Marines* to reflect the fighting style of the Legion.

ARTEFACTS OF THE ALPHA LEGION

Page 75 presents a collection of infamous Relics of the Legion. If your army is led by a Chaos Space Marine Warlord, you can give one of these Artefacts of Chaos to an ALPHA LEGION CHARACTER model from your army, instead of those

found elsewhere in this publication and in other publications.

Note that some weapons replace one of the character's existing weapons. Where this is the case, you must, if you are playing a matched play game or are otherwise using points values, still pay the cost of the weapon that is being replaced. Write down any Artefacts of Chaos your models have on your army roster.

TACTICAL OBJECTIVES

Page 76 provides new Tactical Objectives for use in Maelstrom of War missions to represent the strategies and tactics of the Legion on the battlefield.

NAME GENERATOR

On page 77 you will find a useful tool to help you forge a name for mighty warriors of your Legion, further building the background and personality of your army.

> 'All goes as planned. With this victory, you have sealed your own fate. Look to the horizon, golden warrior, and see your cities burn. The Hydra descends!'
>
> - Trivorius, speaking at the Battle of Lhasnor Gate

ALPHA LEGION WARLORD TRAITS

If an ALPHA LEGION CHARACTER model is your Warlord, you can generate a Warlord Trait from the following table instead of the one from the *Warhammer 40,000* rulebook or *Codex: Chaos Space Marines*. You can either roll one D6 on the table below to randomly generate a Warlord Trait, or you can select the one that best suits your Warlord's preferred style of waging war.

D6 WARLORD TRAIT

1 I AM ALPHARIUS

The Alpha Legion are experts in the art of deception, and none more so than this warlord.

In addition to this Warlord Trait, this Warlord has one randomly generated Chaos Space Marine Warlord Trait from *Codex: Chaos Space Marines*. If this Warlord is destroyed, you can immediately select another ALPHA LEGION CHARACTER model from your army to take their place and generate a Warlord Trait for them (including this one). If the mission you are playing grants victory points for destroying the enemy Warlord, your opponent will only achieve that objective if all of the ALPHA LEGION CHARACTER models from your army have been destroyed.

2 CLANDESTINE

This warlord blends in with his surroundings effortlessly, an esteemed agent with infiltration experience.

When resolving an attack made against this Warlord, subtract 1 from the hit roll.

3 HEADHUNTER

No target is safe in the sights of this warlord.

This Warlord can target CHARACTER units even if they are not the closest enemy unit. When resolving an attack made with a ranged weapon by this Warlord, an unmodified hit roll of 6 inflicts 1 mortal wound on the target in

4 MASTER OF DIVERSION

A venerated tactician who makes use of feints and diversions in their battle plans.

At the start of the first battle round, before the first turn begins, select up to three other friendly ALPHA LEGION units on the battlefield. Remove these units from the battlefield and set them up again following the usual deployment rules for those units and the mission. If you redeploy a TRANSPORT model, all units embarked inside it remain so when it is set up again.

5 CULT LEADER

This warlord directs the local cult personally.

When resolving an attack made with a weapon by a model in a friendly ALPHA LEGION CHAOS CULTIST unit within 6" of this Warlord, on an unmodified wound roll of 6 the Armour Penetration characteristic of that weapon is improved by 1 for that attack (e.g. AP 0 becomes AP -1).

6 FACELESS COMMANDER

This warlord makes use of doubles and proxies to mask their position on the battlefield.

Once per battle, at the end of your Movement phase, you can remove this Warlord from the battlefield and set them up again within 3" of a friendly ALPHA LEGION INFANTRY unit and more than 9" away from enemy models.

ALPHA LEGION STRATAGEMS

If your army is Battle-forged and includes any ALPHA LEGION Detachments (excluding Auxiliary Support Detachments), you have access to the Stratagems shown here.

FORWARD OPERATIVES
1CP

Alpha Legion Stratagem
The Alpha Legion are as illusive as a shadow.

Use this Stratagem during deployment, when you set up an ALPHA LEGION INFANTRY unit from your army. At the start of the first battle round but before the first turn begins, you can move that unit up to 9". It cannot end this move within 9" of any enemy models. If both players have units that can move before the first turn begins, the player who is taking the first turn moves their units first. Each unit can only be selected for this Stratagem once per battle.

CONCEAL
2CP

Alpha Legion Stratagem
These clandestine warriors will disappear at a moment's notice.

Use this Stratagem at the start of your opponent's Shooting phase. Select one ALPHA LEGION INFANTRY unit from your army. Until the end of that phase, enemy models can only target that unit if it is the closest visible target.

SABOTAGED ARMOURY
1CP

Alpha Legion Stratagem
Agents and saboteurs will infiltrate enemy targets long before their warriors join the field of battle.

Use this Stratagem in any phase, before your opponent rolls to see if a VEHICLE model from their army explodes. If any ALPHA LEGION units from your army are on the battlefield, add 3 to one of the D6 rolled, and the roll cannot be re-rolled.

SCRAMBLED COORDINATES
1CP

Alpha Legion Stratagem
Landing co-ordinates are tampered with by infiltrating the enemy's vox and data networks.

Use this Stratagem in your opponent's Movement phase, when an enemy unit is set up on the battlefield as reinforcements but before it is placed on the battlefield. That unit must be set up more than 12" away from ALPHA LEGION units from your army, rather than 9".

RENASCENT INFILTRATION
1CP

Alpha Legion Stratagem
Disappear and reappear for the final strike.

Use this Stratagem at the end of your Movement phase. Select one ALPHA LEGION INFANTRY unit from your army that is more than 3" away from any enemy models (you cannot select a unit that arrived as reinforcements this turn). Remove that unit from the battlefield. At the end of your next Movement phase, set up that unit on the battlefield again, anywhere that is more than 9" away from any enemy models. Any models that cannot be set up in this way are destroyed. If the battle ends before that unit is set back up, it is destroyed.

AMBUSH
2CP

Alpha Legion Stratagem
The Hydra knows all.

Use this Stratagem in your opponent's Movement phase, after an enemy unit is set up on the battlefield as reinforcements. Select one ALPHA LEGION unit from your army within 18" of that unit to shoot at that unit as if it were your Shooting phase.

FEIGNED RETREAT
1CP

Alpha Legion Stratagem
Trust not appearances – the Hydra is always ready to strike.

Use this Stratagem in your Movement phase, when you Fall Back with an ALPHA LEGION unit from your army. That unit can still shoot this turn.

WE ARE ALPHARIUS
1CP

Alpha Legion Stratagem
All Legionnaires can assume the role of leader.

Use this Stratagem before the battle, after nominating your Warlord. Select one ALPHA LEGION CHARACTER model from your army that is not your Warlord and determine one Warlord Trait for it; it is regarded as your Warlord for the purposes of that Warlord Trait. Each Warlord Trait in your army must be unique (if randomly generated, re-roll duplicate results). You can only use this Stratagem once per battle.

ARTEFACTS OF THE ALPHA LEGION

If your army is led by a Chaos Space Marine Warlord, you can give one of these Artefacts of Chaos to an ALPHA LEGION CHARACTER in your army, instead of other Artefacts of Chaos presented elsewhere.

DRAKESCALE PLATE

A suit of Corvus-Alpha-pattern power armour forged by an ancient tech-savant of the Dark Mechanicum, this battle plate incorporates the living titanium scales of the mica skydrake. Its wearer is so well protected by that elder beast's innate resistance to damage, that even a flamestorm cannon's channelled inferno splashes harmlessly aside, like water from smooth pillars of obsidian.

INFANTRY model only. A model with this Relic has a Save characteristic of 2+. When a model with this Relic would lose a wound as a result of a mortal wound, roll one D6; on a 5+ that wound is not lost.

MINDVEIL

Shimmering with illusion, the Mindveil is a long cloak stitched with the interlocking teeth of Dostoy Prime's chameleonic hydrasharks. So potent are the spells of confusion and dislocation cast upon it that the bearer is accompanied by incorporeal mirages that mirror his appearance. Stranger still, at a chanted command in the Dark Tongue, the wearer's true location and that of his doppelganger can switch places, an instant translocation that leaves his enemies gaping in confusion.

At the start of your Movement phase, if a model with this Relic is on the battlefield, roll 3D6; until the end of that phase, that model's Move characteristic is equal to the result. In the Movement phase, a model with this Relic can move across other models and terrain as if they were not there. In the Charge phase, a model with this Relic can move across other models (other than BUILDINGS) as if they were not there. A model with this Relic can charge in a turn in which they Fall Back.

HYDRA'S WAIL

The Hydra's Wail is a sophisticated jamming device corrupted by the ruinous powers. A burst of directed scrapcode infiltrates the vox networks and the communications devices of the enemy, rendering strategic planning null and void. Its blasts are limited, so ritualistic offerings are needed after each use to replenish its deadly charge.

Once per battle, at the start of the battle round, if a model with this Relic is on the battlefield it can activate the Hydra's Wail. Until the end of the battle round, when your opponent spends Command Points to use a Stratagem, roll one D6; on a 4+ your opponent must spend one extra Command Point to use that Stratagem, or else it has no effect and the Command Points spent so far are lost.

VIPER'S BITE

This ornate boltgun has a wide, serpent head muzzle and a magazine that never seems to run dry. When it fires, it makes no noise louder than a dry hiss, but a cacophony of screams is never far behind. The projectiles it fires glow with acrid green flames, and the energy swathing each bolt is so virulent that they can sizzle through even the ancient war-plate of Terminator-armoured veterans.

Model with combi-bolter only. This Relic replaces a combi-bolter and has the following profile:

WEAPON	RANGE	TYPE	S	AP	D
Viper's Bite	24"	Rapid Fire 2	5	-3	2

HYDRA'S TEETH

The legend goes that these bolt rounds are sentient in the manner of Daemon weapons, and that sorcerous powers have somehow given them a terrible hunger for destruction. Once fired, they seek out fresh victims before exploding in a blast of eye-searing, lung-scorching gas.

Model with a bolt weapon (see page 58) only. The bolt weapons of a model with this Relic are granted the following abilities: Attacks made with this weapon automatically hit the target. This weapon wounds on a 2+ unless it is targeting a VEHICLE or TITANIC unit, in which case it wounds on a 6+. Units do not receive the benefit of cover to their saving throws against attacks made with this weapon.

SHADEBLADE

This blade is rumoured to be of xenos origin. Within its hilt lies unknown cloaking technology that turns the wielder into naught but shadow when in darkness and low light.

Model with power sword or force sword only. This Relic replaces a power sword or force sword and has the following profile:

WEAPON	RANGE	TYPE	S	AP	D
Shadeblade	Melee	Melee	+1	-3	D3

Abilities: When resolving an attack made against the bearer, subtract 1 from the hit roll.

ALPHA LEGION TACTICAL OBJECTIVES

These Tactical Objectives are for use in Maelstrom of War missions to represent the strategies and tactics of the Legion on the battlefield.

If your army is led by an **ALPHA LEGION** Warlord, these Tactical Objectives replace the Capture and Control Tactical Objectives (numbers 11-16) in the *Warhammer 40,000* rulebook. If a mission uses Tactical Objectives, players use the normal rules for using Tactical Objectives with the following exception: when an Alpha Legion player generates a Capture and Control objective (numbers 11-16), they instead generate the corresponding Alpha Legion Tactical Objective, as shown below. Other Tactical Objectives (numbers 21-66) are generated normally.

D66	TACTICAL OBJECTIVE
11	Infiltrate and Subvert
12	Tactical Supremacy
13	Strike From Within
14	Strike off the Head
15	Surround the Enemy
16	Cult Uprising

11 — INFILTRATE AND SUBVERT

Use guile and cunning to infiltrate enemy positions before turning against them.

Score 1 victory point if an **ALPHA LEGION** unit from your army is wholly within the enemy's deployment zone at the end of your turn. If you have at least three **ALPHA LEGION** units from your army wholly within the enemy's deployment zone at the end of your turn, score D3 victory points instead.

Alpha Legion

14 — STRIKE OFF THE HEAD

Unlike the Alpha Legion, the enemy's heads do not grow back...

Score D3 victory points for each enemy **CHARACTER** model that was destroyed as a result of an attack made by an **ALPHA LEGION** model from your army during this turn (to a maximum of 6 victory points).

Alpha Legion

12 — TACTICAL SUPREMACY

Engage and destroy the enemy's most tactically specialised units to ensure overall battlefield dominance.

Score 1 victory point if an enemy unit with the Fast Attack, Flyer or Heavy Support Battlefield Role was destroyed as the result of an attack made by a model from your army this turn.

Alpha Legion

15 — SURROUND THE ENEMY

There are many heads of the Hydra primed to strike from all angles.

Score 1 victory point if you have at least three different **ALPHA LEGION** units from your army wholly within 6" of three different battlefield edges at the end of your turn.

Alpha Legion

13 — STRIKE FROM WITHIN

Secure a crucial target behind the enemy's lines that they foolishly think is safe.

Score D3 victory points if you control an objective marker that is within your opponent's deployment zone at the end of your turn.

Alpha Legion

16 — CULT UPRISING

Let not the Legionnaires pay the price of war when the cult can do tenfold.

Score 1 victory point if an enemy unit was destroyed as a result of an attack made by an **ALPHA LEGION** **CHAOS CULTIST** model from your army this turn.

Alpha Legion

ALPHA LEGION NAME GENERATOR

This section is a tool to help you forge a name for mighty warriors of your Legion, to further build the background and personality of your army. If you wish to randomly generate a name for one of your Alpha Legion warriors, you can roll a D66 and consult the table below. To roll a D66, simply roll two D6, one after the other – the first represents tens, and the second represents digits, giving you a result between 11 and 66.

D66	NAME	D66	NAME
11	Kyphax	11	Sheyr
12	Inigo	12	Dynas
13	Poryn	13	Seed
14	Kaevius	14	Omnessar
15	Admon	15	Siphonian
16	Serax	16	the Whisper
21	Jaego	21	Legion
22	Orphos	22	of the Ghost Code
23	Trago	23	X632
24	Asryk	24	Innirus
25	Eskyrx	25	Yartasz
26	Knivos	26	Dureel
31	Kylan	31	23-7
32	Travyx	32	Trial
33	Armilus	33	Decritus
34	Fedyar	34	Speria
35	Dynan	35	Enigma
36	Xanias	36	Lightfall
41	Thkeln	41	Peritas
42	Turelm	42	Ranko
43	Noraphion	43	Phors
44	Alpharius	44	Korsa
45	Hyssar	45	Valdorius
46	Yeryx	46	Phalorin
51	Askelitar	51	Screed
52	Orron	52	Hertzor
53	Tallir	53	Echo
54	Retryn	54	Sygnus
55	Helon	55	Nul
56	Parassus	56	Altorex
61	Zedrak	61	Meerus
62	Sylas	62	Alacrax
63	Zeel	63	Vernius
64	Hammar	64	Anastus
65	Cronyx	65	Korrus
66	Sheed	66	Valpurnius

IRON WARRIORS

In this section you'll find rules for Battle-forged armies that include Iron Warriors Detachments – that is, any Detachment that includes only Iron Warriors units. These include a series of Warlord Traits, Stratagems, Artefacts of Chaos and Tactical Objectives. Together, these reflect the character and fighting style of the Iron Warriors in your games of Warhammer 40,000.

INTRODUCTION

The rules presented in this section are intended to be used in addition to those presented in *Codex: Chaos Space Marines* if you have chosen to take any Iron Warriors Detachments. An Iron Warriors Detachment is still treated as a Chaos Space Marine Detachment for the purposes of the Stratagems, Artefacts of Chaos and Warlord Traits presented in *Codex: Chaos Space Marines*. The following additional rules apply:

Warlord Traits

If an Iron Warriors Character model is your Warlord, you can use the Warlord Traits table on the page opposite instead of those found in other publications to determine what Warlord Trait they have. These allow you to tailor your Warlord to display the typical traits of the leaders of the Legion.

Stratagems

If your army is Battle-forged and includes any Iron Warriors Detachments, the Stratagems on page 80 can be used in addition to those presented in *Codex: Chaos Space Marines* to reflect the fighting style of the Legion.

Artefacts of the Iron Warriors

Page 81 presents a collection of infamous Relics of the Legion. If your army is led by a Chaos Space Marine Warlord, you can give one of these Artefacts of Chaos to an Iron Warriors Character model from your army, instead of those found elsewhere in this publication and in other publications.

Note that some weapons replace one of the character's existing weapons. Where this is the case, you must, if you are playing a matched play game or are otherwise using points values, still pay the cost of the weapon that is being replaced. Write down any Artefacts of Chaos your models have on your army roster.

Tactical Objectives

Page 82 provides new Tactical Objectives for use in Maelstrom of War missions to represent the strategies and tactics of the Legion on the battlefield.

NAME GENERATOR

On page 83 you will find a useful tool to help you forge a name for mighty warriors of your Legion, further building the background and personality of your army.

> 'Huddle close to your Emperor if he makes you feel safe. He cannot save you, for only Chaos is eternal.'
>
> *- Endemion, Captain of the Iron Warriors*

IRON WARRIORS WARLORD TRAITS

If an IRON WARRIORS CHARACTER model is your Warlord, you can generate a Warlord Trait from the following table instead of the one from the *Warhammer 40,000* rulebook or *Codex: Chaos Space Marines*. You can either roll on the table below to randomly generate a Warlord Trait, or you can select the one that best suits your Warlord's preferred style of waging war.

D6   WARLORD TRAIT

1   COLD AND BITTER

The warlords of the Iron Warriors have little room for emotion left in their souls, driven only by bitterness and ruthless efficiency.

When a Morale test is taken for a friendly IRON WARRIORS unit within 6" of this Warlord, do not roll the dice; it is automatically passed.

2   DAEMONSMITH

This warlord has an innate understanding of the relationship between the Daemon and the machine, and will use this to its full potential on the battlefield.

When resolving an attack made by a model in a friendly IRON WARRIORS DAEMON ENGINE or IRON WARRIORS CULT OF DESTRUCTION unit within 6" of this Warlord, an unmodified hit roll of 6 scores 1 additional hit.

3   IRON WITHOUT

Bionics, battle damage and countless scars adorn this warlord, all marking incidents that would have felled lesser warriors.

When this Warlord would lose a

4   BASTION

This warlord is a prime bulwark builder. Any and all available positions are bolstered by fortifications and ramparts.

When resolving an attack made with a weapon that has an Armour Penetration characteristic of -1 against a friendly IRON WARRIORS unit that is within 6" of this Warlord and receiving the benefit of cover, that weapon is treated as having an Armour Penetration characteristic of 0.

5   SIEGE MASTER

When a heavily defended position needs nothing short of ceaseless firepower, this warlord will deliver.

When resolving an attack made with a ranged weapon by a model in a friendly IRON WARRIORS HAVOCS or IRON WARRIORS VEHICLE unit within 6" of this Warlord, re-roll a wound roll of 1.

6   STOIC ADVANCE

This warlord advances with bitter resolve and, by his example, his followers do the same.

'I want this fortress pulverised. I want no stone left standing atop another. I want to watch those loyalist dogs crawl, weeping from the rubble, and I want to crush their wretched skulls beneath my boot. See it done.'

- *Lord Magrax Earthbreaker of the Iron Warriors*

IRON WARRIORS STRATAGEMS

If your army is Battle-forged and includes any IRON WARRIORS Detachments (excluding Auxiliary Support Detachments), you have access to the Stratagems shown here.

IRON WITHIN, IRON WITHOUT
1CP

Iron Warriors Stratagem

Hardened by the most gruelling theatres of war, the Iron Warriors will fight long after others of their ilk have fallen.

Use this Stratagem in any phase, when a model in an **IRON WARRIORS** unit from your army would lose a wound. Roll one D6 for that wound, and for each other wound that would be lost by a model in that unit until the end of that phase; on a 6 that wound is not lost.

TANK HUNTERS
1CP

Iron Warriors Stratagem

No armour is safe from the guns of the IV Legion.

Use this Stratagem in your Shooting phase or the Fight phase, when you choose an **IRON WARRIORS** unit from your army (excluding **CHAOS CULTISTS**) to shoot or fight with. Select one enemy **VEHICLE** unit. Until the end of that phase, when resolving an attack made by a model in that **IRON WARRIORS** unit against the selected unit, you can re-roll the wound roll.

METHODICAL ANNIHILATION
1CP

Iron Warriors Stratagem

With meticulous firepower do the Iron Warriors prevail.
Use this Stratagem in your Shooting phase, when an **IRON WARRIORS** unit from your army is chosen to shoot with. Select one of the following effects to last until the end of that phase:
- When resolving an attack made by a model in that unit, you can re-roll the damage roll.
- You can re-roll any or all of the dice to determine the Type characteristic of weapons that models in that unit are equipped with.

RAMPANT TECHNO-VIRUS
1CP

Iron Warriors Stratagem

The IV's Cult of Destruction are fearsome avatars of war.

Use this Stratagem in your Shooting phase or the Fight phase, when you select an **IRON WARRIORS OBLITERATORS** or **IRON WARRIORS MUTILATORS** unit from your army to shoot or fight with. Until the end of that phase, you can re-roll any or all D3 rolls made for that unit's Fleshmetal Guns or Fleshmetal Weapons ability.

CANNON FODDER
2GP

Iron Warriors Stratagem

Clog up their guns with the flesh and bones of the weak.

Use this Stratagem at the start of your opponent's Shooting phase. Select one **IRON WARRIORS INFANTRY** unit from your army then select one friendly **IRON WARRIORS CHAOS CULTISTS** unit wholly within 6" of that unit. Until the end of that phase, enemy models cannot target that **IRON WARRIORS INFANTRY** unit if the selected **IRON WARRIORS CHAOS CULTISTS** unit is a closer visible target.

DOUR DUTY
1CP

Iron Warriors Stratagem

The Iron Warriors unflinchingly face their forlorn fate.

Use this Stratagem in your opponent's Shooting phase or your Charge phase, when an **IRON WARRIORS** unit from your army is chosen as the target for an attack. Until the end of that phase, when resolving an attack made with a ranged weapon against that unit, worsen the Armour Penetration characteristic of that weapon by 1 for that attack (e.g. AP -1 becomes AP 0).

BITTER ENMITY
1CP

Iron Warriors Stratagem

The IV's contempt for the Imperial Fists runs deep.

Use this Stratagem in the Fight phase, when an **IRON WARRIORS** unit from your army is chosen to fight with. Until the end of that phase, when resolving an attack made with a melee weapon by a model in that unit against an **IMPERIAL FISTS** unit, you can re-roll the hit roll and you can re-roll the wound roll.

UNHOLY VIGOUR
1CP

Iron Warriors Stratagem

The corrupted machine spirits of the IV refuse to yield.

Use this Stratagem at the start of your Movement phase. Select one **IRON WARRIORS VEHICLE** model from your army. That model regains up to 3 lost wounds.

ARTEFACTS OF THE IRON WARRIORS

If your army is led by a Chaos Space Marine Warlord, you can give one of these Artefacts of Chaos to an Iron Warriors Character model from your army, instead of other Artefacts of Chaos presented elsewhere.

SIEGEBREAKER MACE

A vast sphere of dense star-metal bound with sigils of shattering, the Siegebreaker Mace, mounted on the wrist-thick pole of a captured Adeptus Astartes standard, was created with acts of destructive symbolism in mind.

Model with power maul or accursed crozius only. This Relic replaces a power maul or accursed crozius and has the following profile:

WEAPON	RANGE	TYPE	S	AP	D
Siegebreaker Mace	When the bearer fights, select one of the profiles below.				
- Swing	Melee	Melee	+2	-2	2
- Smash	Melee	Melee	x2	-3	D6

Abilities: When the bearer fights using the smash profile, it can only make two attacks. When resolving an attack made with the smash profile, roll two D6 when inflicting damage with it and discard one of the results.

CRANIUM MALEVOLUS

This iron-clad death's head is a mouthpiece for the mind shattering language of the soul forges. The coded blurts of Dark Tongue it emits are potent enough to undo the machine spirits of enemy technology.

In your Shooting phase, a model with this Relic can use the Cranium Malevolus instead of shooting. Roll one D6 for each enemy Vehicle unit within 9" of that model; on a 4-5 that unit suffers D3 mortal wounds, and on a 6 that unit suffers 3 mortal wounds.

INSIDIUM

This vast suite of bionics was originally implanted to avoid the mutating effects of the immaterium, but the warp is fickle. Insidium and its bearer are now a warped host of the techno-virus. Flesh and bionic alike have melded into a sickening union of mutated horror, while the bearer's disdain for their own corruption rots away at their soul. Nonetheless, a fusion of mortal, Daemon and machine has turned them into an unstoppable leviathan.

A model with this Relic gains the Daemon keyword (if it does not already have it). Add 1 to the Strength, Toughness and Wounds characteristics of that model.

AXE OF THE FORGEMASTER

Masters of the Daemon forges have long had to ensure dominance over their creations. Such are the energies of unmaking bound into this axe's haft that a single blow can turn an adamantium-hulled tank into a pile of rusted scrap.

Model with power axe or daemonic axe only. This Relic replaces a power axe or daemonic axe and has the following profile:

WEAPON	RANGE	TYPE	S	AP	D
Axe of the Forgemaster	Melee	Melee	+3	-3	2

Abilities: When resolving an attack made with this weapon against a Vehicle unit, an unmodified hit roll of 5+ inflicts D3 mortal wounds on the target in addition to any normal damage.

SPITESPITTER

The unbridled hate of this weapon's various wielders has corrupted its spirit over 10,000 years in the warp. The weapon now bucks with venom from every round that leaves its chamber, an essence of loathing that trails the explosive casing. For each loyal servant of the Corpse Emperor destroyed, this weapon and its wielder make one small step towards victory in the Long War.

Model with combi-bolter only. This Relic replaces a combi-bolter and has the following profile:

WEAPON	RANGE	TYPE	S	AP	D
Spitespitter	24"	Rapid Fire 2	5	-3	D3

TECHNO-VENOMOUS MECHATENDRILS

The morass of mechanical tentacles that grace the wearer's back are possessed of an insidious and cruel consciousness, for they are a collection of several small and deadly Daemon Engines.

Warpsmith model only. This Relic replaces mechatendrils and has the following profile:

WEAPON	RANGE	TYPE	S	AP	D
Techno-venomous Mechatendrils	Melee	Melee	User	0	1

Abilities: When the bearer fights, it makes 4 additional attacks with this weapon, and only those 4 attacks can be made with this weapon. When resolving an attack made with this weapon, if a hit is scored the target suffers 1 mortal wound and the attack sequence ends.

IRON WARRIORS TACTICAL OBJECTIVES

These Tactical Objectives are for use in Maelstrom of War missions to represent the strategies and tactics of the Legion on the battlefield.

If your army is led by an **IRON WARRIORS** Warlord, these Tactical Objectives replace the Capture and Control Tactical Objectives (numbers 11-16) in the *Warhammer 40,000* rulebook. If a mission uses Tactical Objectives, players use the normal rules for using Tactical Objectives with the following exception: when an Iron Warriors player generates a Capture and Control objective (numbers 11-16), they instead generate the corresponding Iron Warriors Tactical Objective, as shown below. Other Tactical Objectives (numbers 21-66) are generated normally.

D66	TACTICAL OBJECTIVE
11	Repel Invaders
12	Tactical Destruction
13	Wanton Obliteration
14	Hold and Fortify
15	Masters of Demolition
16	Destroy Their Armoury

11 — REPEL INVADERS

An Iron Warriors battle line is an unbreachable fortress.

Score D3 victory points if an enemy unit wholly within your deployment zone was destroyed as a result of an attack made by an **IRON WARRIORS** model from your army this turn.

Iron Warriors

12 — TACTICAL DESTRUCTION

The enemy seeks to hold a valuable position against you. Attest to their folly by annihilating them.

Score 1 victory point for each enemy unit controlling an objective marker at the start of the turn that was destroyed as a result of an attack made by an **IRON WARRIORS** model from your army this turn (to a maximum of 6 victory points).

Iron Warriors

13 — WANTON OBLITERATION

Prove the superiority of the techno-virus by using it to ensure the foe's annihilation.

Score 1 victory point if an enemy unit was destroyed as a result of an attack made by an **IRON WARRIORS CULT OF DESTRUCTION** or **IRON WARRIORS DAEMON ENGINE** model from your army this turn.

Iron Warriors

14 — HOLD AND FORTIFY

Hold this crucial position and let none dispute your control of it.

When this Tactical Objective is generated, nominate one objective marker. Score D3 victory points if you control that objective marker at the end of your next turn (or at the end of the game).

Iron Warriors

15 — MASTERS OF DEMOLITION

The Iron Warriors have no equal when it comes to demolition.

Score 1 victory point if an enemy unit entirely on or within a terrain feature, or an enemy **BUILDING** model, was destroyed as a result of an attack made by an **IRON WARRIORS** model from your army this turn.

Iron Warriors

16 — DESTROY THEIR ARMOURY

Without vehicle support, the enemy's strength is nothing compared to your own.

Score 1 victory point if an enemy **VEHICLE** model was destroyed as a result of an attack made by an **IRON WARRIORS** model from your army this turn. If an enemy **TITANIC** model was destroyed as a result of an attack made by an **IRON WARRIORS** model from your army this turn, score D3 victory points instead.

Iron Warriors

IRON WARRIORS NAME GENERATOR

This section is a tool to help you forge a name for mighty warriors of your Legion, to further build the background and personality of your army. If you wish to randomly generate a name for one of your Iron Warriors, you can roll a D66 and consult the table below. To roll a D66, simply roll two D6, one after the other – the first represents tens and the second represents digits, giving you a result between 11 and 66.

D66	NAME
11	Ferrox
12	Rannok
13	Attrax
14	Sulphus
15	Quixus
16	Sullus
21	Etrog
22	Tarrax
23	Drar
24	Tarnax
25	Herdax
26	Crol
31	Dreddusk
32	Varsigonn
33	Illux
34	Vonnax
35	Porso
36	Orn
41	Harram
42	Norros
43	Endion
44	Paradus
45	Sever
46	Dorgus
51	Lotros
52	Porox
53	Orim
54	Broug
55	Semnex
56	Ossus
61	Khyr
62	Ummek
63	Vhegor
64	Barxok
65	Hama
66	Detrus

D66	NAME
11	the Unmaker
12	Destorax
13	Bharrox
14	Vhaxxan
15	Metagor
16	the Wallbreaker
21	Tarlensus
22	Estarox
23	Gorn
24	the Warpcutter
25	Kharaxiani
26	the Shatterer
31	of Praxas
32	Toramini
33	Veszrax
34	Korpanos
35	Zhorisch
36	Anarax
41	Kron-tu
42	Parrtox
43	Hrendor
44	Nassour
45	Taclimor
46	of Netremor
51	Ommorex
52	Falkos
53	Vorpasian
54	of the Foundry
55	Shon-tu
56	Hansao
61	Dronn
62	Gan-rus
63	Shon-tar
64	Steelspine
65	Rustclaw
66	Erdalexi

EMPEROR'S CHILDREN

In this section you'll find rules for Battle-forged armies that include EMPEROR'S CHILDREN Detachments – that is, any Detachment that includes only EMPEROR'S CHILDREN units. These include a series of Warlord Traits, Stratagems, Artefacts of Chaos and Tactical Objectives. Together, these reflect the character and fighting style of the Emperor's Children in your games of Warhammer 40,000.

INTRODUCTION

The rules presented in this section are intended to be used in addition to those presented in *Codex: Chaos Space Marines* if you have chosen to take any EMPEROR'S CHILDREN Detachments. An EMPEROR'S CHILDREN Detachment is still treated as a Chaos Space Marine Detachment for the purposes of the Stratagems, Artefacts of Chaos and Warlord Traits presented in *Codex: Chaos Space Marines*. The following additional rules apply:

CHARACTER model from your army, instead of those found elsewhere in this publication and in other publications.

Note that some weapons replace one of the character's existing weapons. Where this is the case, you must, if you are playing a matched play game or are otherwise using points values, still pay the cost of the weapon that is being replaced. Write down any Artefacts of Chaos your models have on your army roster.

WARLORD TRAITS

If an EMPEROR'S CHILDREN CHARACTER model is your Warlord, you can use the Warlord Traits table on the page opposite instead of those found in other publications to determine what Warlord Trait they have. These allow you to tailor your Warlord to display the typical traits of the leaders of the Legion.

'Thrill in the noise that breaks the skin and ravages the mind! Savour the shuddering, shaking screams that shiver the spine and shatter the skull. Let sensation wash over you, through you, claim you and cast you aside!'

- Bellerophid,
Scarlet Marquis of the
Emperor's Children

STRATAGEMS

If your army is Battle-forged and includes any EMPEROR'S CHILDREN Detachments, the Stratagems on page 86 can be used in addition to those presented in *Codex: Chaos Space Marines* to reflect the fighting style of the Legion.

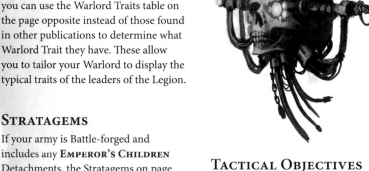

TACTICAL OBJECTIVES

Page 88 provides new Tactical Objectives for use in Maelstrom of War missions to represent the strategies and tactics of the Legion on the battlefield.

ARTEFACTS OF THE EMPEROR'S CHILDREN

Page 87 presents a collection of infamous Relics of the Legion. If your army is led by a Chaos Space Marine Warlord, you can give one of these Artefacts of Chaos to an EMPEROR'S CHILDREN

NAME GENERATOR

On page 89 you will find a useful tool to help you forge a name for mighty warriors of your Legion, further building the background and personality of your army.

EMPEROR'S CHILDREN WARLORD TRAITS

If an EMPEROR'S CHILDREN CHARACTER model is your Warlord, you can generate a Warlord Trait from the following table instead of the one from the *Warhammer 40,000* rulebook or *Codex: Chaos Space Marines*. You can either roll on the table below to randomly generate a Warlord Trait, or you can select the one that best suits your Warlord's preferred style of waging war.

D6 WARLORD TRAIT

1 STIMULATED BY PAIN
The warlords of the Emperor's Children thrive on pain. The more grievous their injuries, the deadlier they become.

Add 1 to your Warlord's Attacks characteristic for each wound he has suffered (to a maximum of +3). If your Warlord regains any lost wounds, he loses the associated bonus attacks.

2 INTOXICATING MUSK
A sickly-sweet aroma emanates from this warlord, both delightful and disgusting at once. A perfumed assault on the senses intoxicates those in its vicinity.

When resolving an attack made by an enemy unit within 3" of this Warlord, subtract 1 from the hit roll.

3 UNBOUND ARROGANCE
This warlord's pride and hubris is both his greatest strength and his biggest weakness.

When you choose this Warlord to fight with, you and your opponent secretly choose a number from 1 to 3 on a D6 (we suggest turning a D6 to show the number but concealing this behind your hand), then reveal your choice simultaneously. If the chosen numbers differ, this Warlord can make a number of additional attacks that fight sequence equal to the number you chose.

4 FAULTLESS DUELLIST
A veteran of the duel, a peerless swordsman and an exquisite example of fighting form. Those who lock swords with this warlord do so at their peril.

At the start of the Fight phase, roll one D3. Until the end of that phase, subtract the result from the Attacks characteristic of enemy models (to a minimum of 1) whilst they are within 1" of this Warlord.

5 GLUTTON FOR PUNISHMENT
This warlord revels in every sensation - even ones that would slay a lesser mortal outright.

When resolving an attack against this Warlord, reduce any damage inflicted by 1 (to a minimum of 1).

6 LOATHSOME GRACE
Blessed by the Chaos Gods to further accentuate this warlord's perverse elegance, his warped movements are nimble, striking and utterly abhorrent.

When a charge roll is made for this Warlord, you can re-roll the dice. If this Warlord makes a charge move or performs a Heroic Intervention, add 1 to their Strength and Attacks characteristics until the end of the subsequent Fight phase.

> 'My gift to you is pure and unalloyed sensation. Embrace the exquisite agony, my friend. Let it course into your veins and burn away your doubt and your weakness, leaving nothing but transcendent bliss behind. Should you survive, you will fall to your knees and give me thanks.'
>
> - Lord Fulmenes of the Mirrorhost

EMPEROR'S CHILDREN STRATAGEMS

If your army is Battle-forged and includes any EMPEROR'S CHILDREN Detachments (excluding Auxiliary Support Detachments), you have access to the Stratagems shown here.

COMBAT ELIXIRS
2CP

Emperor's Children Stratagem
Concoctions of hideous euphoria empower the minds of these sensationalist warriors.

Use this Stratagem before the battle. Select one EMPEROR'S CHILDREN unit from your army that is not a VEHICLE or CHAOS CULTIST, then select one of the following effects to apply to models in that unit until the end of the battle:

- +1 to Attacks characteristic
- +1 to Strength characteristic
- +2" to Move characteristic
- +1 to Toughness characteristic

You can only use this Stratagem once per battle.

EXCESS OF VIOLENCE
1CP

Emperor's Children Stratagem
The visceral sensation of every fresh kill causes the warriors of the Emperor's Children to enter an ecstatic frenzy of butchery and dismemberment.

Use this Stratagem in the Fight phase, when you choose an EMPEROR'S CHILDREN INFANTRY unit from your army to fight with. Until the end of that phase, if an attack made by a model in that unit destroys an enemy model, the attacking model can make one additional attack against the same unit using the same weapon.

INCESSANT DISDAIN
1CP

Emperor's Children Stratagem
Contempt for lesser warriors drives the Champions of the Emperor's Children into a furore.

Use this Stratagem at the end of your opponent's Charge phase. Select one EMPEROR'S CHILDREN CHARACTER model from your army. That model can perform a Heroic Intervention if it is within 6" of any enemy models, and can move up to 6" when doing so as long as it finishes that move within 1" of any enemy CHARACTER models or the nearest enemy model.

HONOUR THE PRINCE
1CP

Emperor's Children Stratagem
Warriors who venerate Slaanesh through fighting form are rewarded in their endeavours.

Use this Stratagem in your Charge phase, after making a charge roll for an EMPEROR'S CHILDREN SLAANESH unit from your army. You can change the result of one of the D6 rolled to a 6.

EXCRUCIATING FREQUENCIES
1CP

Emperor's Children Stratagem
The sons of Chemos were the first to use sonic weaponry, and are peerless with its deadly sound waves.

Use this Stratagem in your Shooting phase, when an EMPEROR'S CHILDREN NOISE MARINES unit from your army is chosen to shoot with. Until the end of that phase, add 1 to the Strength and Damage characteristics of blastmasters, sonic blasters and doom sirens models in that unit are equipped with.

CRUEL DUELLISTS
1CP

Emperor's Children Stratagem
Fulgrim's scions are renowned for their blade-craft.

Use this Stratagem in the Fight phase, when an EMPEROR'S CHILDREN unit from your army that is not a VEHICLE or CHAOS CULTIST is chosen to fight with. Until the end of that phase, when resolving an attack made with a melee weapon by a model in that unit, on an unmodified wound roll of 6 that weapon has an Armour Penetration characteristic of -3 for that attack.

TACTICAL PERFECTION
1CP

Emperor's Children Stratagem
The III Legion's grasp of tactics is exemplary.

Use this Stratagem at the start of the first battle round, before the first turn begins. Select one EMPEROR'S CHILDREN unit from your army. Remove that unit from the battlefield and set it up again following the usual deployment rules for that unit and the mission being played. If you redeploy a TRANSPORT model, units embarked aboard it remain so when it is set up again.

ARTEFACTS OF THE EMPEROR'S CHILDREN

If your army is led by a Chaos Space Marine Warlord, you can give one of these Artefacts of Chaos to an EMPEROR'S CHILDREN CHARACTER model from your army, instead of other Artefacts of Chaos presented elsewhere.

THE ENDLESS GRIN

This fleshy mask is the still living, flayed face of a man who begged Slaanesh to fulfil his wish to live forever. The Dark Prince was only too pleased to oblige, gifting the unfortunate soul immortality, but also forcing him to present his face to the Chaos Lord Shixe. After butchering the supplicant, Shixe wore that face as a prized reminder of the occasion for several centuries. The Endless Grin has since exchanged hands many times, but the potency of its anguish has never diminished.

When a Morale test is taken for an enemy unit within 6" of a model with this Relic, your opponent must roll one additional D6 and you can choose one of those dice to be discarded. Subtract 1 from the Leadership characteristic of models in enemy units whilst their unit is within 6" of a model with this Relic.

FATAL SONANCY

Xenotech implants grafted into the bearer's neck give them the ability to emit a hypermodulated scream, powerful enough to shatter diamond. The myriad resonant frequencies and sheer deafening power of this scream hits with a physical impact, blasting away flesh and bone alike, and reducing its victims to a shuddering pulp.

This Relic is a weapon that has the following profile:

WEAPON	RANGE	TYPE	S	AP	D
Fatal Sonancy	12"	Assault D6	6	-2	1

Abilities: When resolving an attack made with this weapon, do not make a hit roll: it automatically scores a hit. When resolving an attack made with this weapon, the target does not receive the benefit of cover to its saving throw.

ARMOUR OF ABHORRENCE

A canvas of the perverse, this suit of armour turns the wearer into an effigy of excess. Captured warriors of the enemy will adorn its plate, a mosaic of dark exuberance that delights the Emperor's Children, but instils sheer horror in their enemies. In battle, warriors experience utter revulsion at the ghastly display, and feel a brief reluctance at firing upon their captured brothers. Before they come to their senses, the bearer is in their midst.

Enemy units cannot fire Overwatch at a model with this Relic. If an enemy unit fails a Morale test whilst it is within 6" of a model with this Relic, one additional model flees from that unit.

REMNANT OF THE MARAVIGLIA

A rare recording of the grand symphony played for the Emperor's Children at the onset of the Horus Heresy. The original performance saw the final descent of the Legion into debauchery and darkness. When transmitted through vox-casters, purpose built into the Dark Apostle's armour, mere seconds of this perverted symphony is enough to drive the servants of Slaanesh into a furore of excess.

PRIEST model only. Once per battle, instead of chanting a prayer, a model with this Relic can broadcast the Remnant of the Maraviglia. Until the end of that battle round, when resolving an attack made by a model in a friendly EMPEROR'S CHILDREN unit within 6" of a model with this Relic, you can re-roll the wound roll.

DISTORTION

The unblemished sheen of this faultless blade reflects an alluring countenance to the bearer, their seemingly unmatched beauty a peerless example of perfection. In reality, the bearer is a hideous wretch, every ounce of elegance leeched away to power the blade's fearsome edge.

Model with power sword or force sword only. This Relic replaces a power sword or force sword and has the following profile:

WEAPON	RANGE	TYPE	S	AP	D
Distortion	Melee	Melee	User	-4	D3

Abilities: At the start of the Fight Phase, the bearer can look upon their reflection. Until the end of that phase, this weapon has a Strength characteristic of x2, and when resolving an attack made with this weapon, subtract 1 from the hit roll.

RAIMENT REVULSIVE

A cloak stitched with the skins of defeated mortals, the Raiment Revulsive is a symbol of contempt and hatred for those lesser than the Emperor's Children. The screams of anguish that come from the still living faces of its diabolic hide are a sweet concerto to the ears of the wearer. It imbues them with unbridled confidence in their ability to best enemies, flay their hides in victory, and add their still screaming throes to the length of this grisly mantle.

When resolving an attack made by a model with this Relic, you can re-roll the hit roll and you can re-roll the wound roll. When a charge roll is made for a model with this Relic, you can re-roll the result.

EMPEROR'S CHILDREN TACTICAL OBJECTIVES

These Tactical Objectives are for use in Maelstrom of War missions to represent the strategies and tactics of the Legion on the battlefield.

If your army is led by an **EMPEROR'S CHILDREN** Warlord, these Tactical Objectives replace the Capture and Control Tactical Objectives (numbers 11-16) in the *Warhammer 40,000* rulebook. If a mission uses Tactical Objectives, players use the normal rules for using Tactical Objectives with the following exception: when an Emperor's Children player generates a Capture and Control objective (numbers 11-16), they instead generate the corresponding Emperor's Children Tactical Objective, as shown below. Other Tactical Objectives (numbers 21-66) are generated normally.

D66	TACTICAL OBJECTIVE
11	The Sound of Death
12	Without Peer
13	Taste of Despair
14	That Which They Value Most
15	Flawless Performance
16	For the Dark Prince

11 — THE SOUND OF DEATH

Few can stand up to the wall of sanity-blasting sound emitted by the sonic weapons of the Emperor's Children.

Score 1 victory point if an enemy unit was destroyed this turn as a result of an attack made with a sonic blaster, doom siren or blastmaster by an **EMPEROR'S CHILDREN NOISE MARINE** model from your army.

Emperor's Children

14 — THAT WHICH THEY VALUE MOST

At the core of every Emperor's Children legionary lies a spiteful heart that revels in the despair of others.

When this Tactical Objective is generated, your opponent must choose one objective marker. Score D3 victory points if you control that objective marker at the end of your turn.

Emperor's Children

12 — WITHOUT PEER

Slaanesh demands great deeds of his champions, especially in the field of personal combat.

Score D3 victory points if an enemy **CHARACTER** model was destroyed as a result of an attack made by an **EMPEROR'S CHILDREN** model from your army in the Fight phase of this turn.

Emperor's Children

15 — FLAWLESS PERFORMANCE

Since their foundation, the Emperor's Children have sought to master the art of perfection in warfare.

Score D3+3 victory points if you control four or more objective markers at the end of your turn and your opponent controls no objective markers at the end of your turn.

Emperor's Children

13 — TASTE OF DESPAIR

The Emperor's Children savour the essence of the enemy at their most terrified, when the full, undiluted impact of death surrounds them.

Score 1 victory point if any enemy units failed Morale test whilst within 6" of any **EMPEROR'S CHILDREN** units from your army this turn.

Emperor's Children

16 — FOR THE DARK PRINCE

Exalt Slaanesh in the sensation of battle.

Score 1 victory point if 6 or more enemy models were destroyed as a result of attacks made by a single **EMPEROR'S CHILDREN** unit from your army in any single phase of this turn.

Emperor's Children

EMPEROR'S CHILDREN NAME GENERATOR

This section is a tool to help you forge a name for mighty warriors of your Legion to further build the background and personality of your army. If you wish to randomly generate a name for one of your Emperor's Children warriors, you can roll a D66 and consult the table below. To roll a D66, simply roll two D6, one after the other – the first represents tens, and the second represents digits, giving you a result between 11 and 66.

D66	NAME	D66	NAME
11	Antinius	11	Konemos
12	Choristus	12	Sentrillion
13	Dalian	13	Thastalis
14	Laviscus	14	Thorn
15	Shiron	15	Mirrorborn
16	Adamatar	16	the Perfect
21	Porillion	21	Thest
22	Xiander	22	Vessatar
23	Abdemis	23	Cathonian
24	Travolian	24	Kelemnid
25	Sperios	25	Bericosian
26	Fabian	26	Xandassus
31	Haxamel	31	Tresell
32	Eidar	32	Vairoscan
33	Eidelitor	33	Demetrius
34	Yorios	34	Kaesoron
35	Hurillon	35	of the Silken Blade
36	Retigarius	36	the Idolator
41	Julianis	41	the Hedonist
42	Posca	42	Alkenex
43	Glabius	43	the Seeker of Pleasures
44	Aloysian	44	Fortillian
45	Ilitoias	45	Kanasiar
46	Xuvis	46	Raescidus
51	Amasced	51	Quiridian
52	Dellinus	52	the Inevitable
53	Hascule	53	Capersi
54	Xiortes	54	Iollus
55	Lucian	55	Vastorian
56	Saul	56	Nemoleth
61	Teloss	61	Aquillian
62	Clavius	62	Calarus
63	Decanus	63	Fortesian
64	Grythan	64	Peristoclade
65	Lycon	65	Ryllaneus
66	Solomon	66	Ketoris

WORLD EATERS

In this section you'll find rules for Battle-forged armies that include WORLD EATERS Detachments – that is, any Detachment that includes only WORLD EATERS units. These include a series of Warlord Traits, Stratagems, Artefacts of Chaos and Tactical Objectives. Together, these reflect the character and fighting style of the World Eaters in your games of Warhammer 40,000.

INTRODUCTION

The rules presented in this section are intended to be used in addition to those presented in *Codex: Chaos Space Marines* if you have chosen to take any WORLD EATERS Detachments. A WORLD EATERS Detachment is still treated as a Chaos Space Marine Detachment for the purposes of the Stratagems, Artefacts of Chaos and Warlord Traits presented in *Codex: Chaos Space Marines*. The following additional rules apply:

WARLORD TRAITS

If a WORLD EATERS CHARACTER model is your Warlord, you can use the Warlord Traits table on the page opposite instead of those found in other publications to determine what Warlord Trait they have. These allow you to tailor your Warlord to display the typical traits of the leaders of the Legion.

STRATAGEMS

If your army is Battle-forged and includes any WORLD EATERS Detachments, the Stratagems on page 92 can be used in addition to those presented in *Codex: Chaos Space Marines* to reflect the fighting style of the Legion.

ARTEFACTS OF THE WORLD EATERS

Page 93 presents a collection of infamous Relics of the Legion. If your army is led by a Chaos Space Marine Warlord, you can give one of these Artefacts of Chaos to a WORLD EATERS CHARACTER model from your army, instead of those

found elsewhere in this publication and in other publications.

Note that some weapons replace one of the character's existing weapons. Where this is the case, you must, if you are playing a matched play game or are otherwise using points values, still pay the cost of the weapon that is being replaced. Write down any Artefacts of Chaos your models have on your army roster.

TACTICAL OBJECTIVES

Page 94 provides new Tactical Objectives for use in Maelstrom of War missions to represent the strategies and tactics of the Legion on the battlefield.

NAME GENERATOR

On page 95 you will find a useful tool to help you forge a name for mighty warriors of your Legion, further building the background and personality of your army.

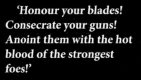

'Honour your blades! Consecrate your guns! Anoint them with the hot blood of the strongest foes!'

- *Darius Khanan, Lord of the Blood Brotherhood*

WORLD EATERS WARLORD TRAITS

If a WORLD EATERS CHARACTER model is your Warlord, you can generate a Warlord Trait from the following table instead of the one from the *Warhammer 40,000* rulebook or *Codex: Chaos Space Marines*. You can either roll on the table below to randomly generate a Warlord Trait, or you can select the one that best suits your Warlord's preferred style of waging war.

D6   WARLORD TRAIT

1   SLAUGHTERBORN

This warlord bears the favour of Khorne, his murderous prowess growing with each worthy skull claimed in his master's name.

When an enemy CHARACTER, MONSTER or TITANIC model is destroyed as a result of an attack made by this Warlord, add 1 to this Warlord's Attacks and Strength characteristics.

2   ARCH SLAUGHTERER

When surrounded by foes to kill, this warlord is truly in his element, and gives in to the Butcher's Nails.

At the start of the Fight phase, add D3 to this Warlord's Attacks characteristic if there are more enemy models within 3" of them than there are friendly models. These extra attacks last until the end of that Fight phase.

3   DISCIPLE OF KHORNE

Many claim to hold the title of one of Khorne's eight foremost champions, but any pretenders are swiftly proven false, for none can rival one of their number in the art of single combat.

When resolving an attack made with a melee weapon by this Warlord against an enemy CHARACTER unit or a unit that contains any models with a Wounds characteristic of 5 or more, you can re-roll the hit roll and you can re-roll the wound roll.

4   VIOLENT URGENCY

This warlord's bloodlust is palpable and pushes the Butcher's Nails of those around him into overdrive. This, in turn, fuels a desperate need to spill blood.

When an Advance or charge roll is made for a friendly WORLD EATERS unit within 6" of this Warlord, add 1 to the result.

5   TRUE BERZERKER

When this warlord meets his foes face-to-face, his fury is such that he will brush aside even fatal wounds, the better to claim more skulls for Lord Khorne.

When resolving an attack made with a melee weapon against this model, halve any damage inflicted (rounding up).

6   BATTLE-LUST

This warlord's lust for battle draws him into any and all fights, his thirst driving him to new heights of battlefield frenzy.

This Warlord can perform a Heroic Intervention if there are any enemy units within 6" of them instead of 3", and when doing so can move up to 6" instead of 3". This Warlord always fights first in the Fight phase even if they didn't charge. If the enemy has units that have charged, or that have a similar ability, then alternate choosing units to fight with, starting with the player whose turn is taking place.

WORLD EATERS STRATAGEMS

If your army is Battle-forged and includes any WORLD EATERS Detachments (excluding Auxiliary Support Detachments), you have access to the Stratagems shown here.

1CP — SCORN OF SORCERY
World Eaters Stratagem
Like the god they worship, the warriors of the World Eaters despise psykers and their trickery, and through the sheer force of their hatred can sever sorcerous powers.

Use this Stratagem in your opponent's Psychic phase, when an enemy PSYKER model manifests a psychic power within 24" of any WORLD EATERS units from your army. Roll one D6; on a 4+ the effects of that psychic power are negated.

1CP — APOPLECTIC FRENZY
World Eaters Stratagem
Howling in rage, World Eaters surge towards the foe.

Use this Stratagem during deployment, when you set up a WORLD EATERS INFANTRY unit from your army. At the start of the first battle round but before the first turn begins, you can move that unit up to 9". It cannot end this move within 9" of any enemy models. If both players have units that can move before the first turn begins, the player who is taking the first turn moves their units first

1CP — SKULLS FOR THE SKULL THRONE!
World Eaters Stratagem
Offer up the skulls of mighty champions to Khorne!

Use this Stratagem in the Fight phase, when an enemy CHARACTER model is destroyed as a result of an attack made with a melee weapon by a WORLD EATERS CHARACTER model from your army. Gain D3 Command Points.

2CP — RED BUTCHERS
World Eaters Stratagem
Entombed within their Terminator armour, these crazed warriors are unleashed like rabid beasts.

Use this Stratagem before the battle. Select one WORLD EATERS CHAOS TERMINATORS unit from your army. Add 1 to the Strength characteristic of models in that unit, and that unit gains the following ability: 'Blood for the Blood God: This unit can fight twice in each Fight phase, instead of only once'. You can only use this Stratagem once per battle.

1CP — KILL! MAIM! BURN!
World Eaters Stratagem
Kill! Maim! Burn! Kill! Maim! Burn! Kill! Maim! Burn!

Use this Stratagem in the Fight phase, before you consolidate with a WORLD EATERS unit from your army. Until the end of that phase, each model in that unit can move up to 6" when they consolidate, instead of 3".

1CP — WILD FURY
World Eaters Stratagem
Sheer aggression can cut through even the thickest armour.

Use this Stratagem in the Fight phase, when you select a WORLD EATERS unit from your army to fight with. Until the end of that phase, improve the Armour Penetration characteristic of melee weapons models in that unit are equipped with by 1 (e.g. AP 0 becomes AP -1).

1CP — STOKE THE NAILS
World Eaters Stratagem
Aggression stimulators implanted into the brains of the World Eaters drive them into uncontrollable rages.

Use this Stratagem in the Fight phase, when a WORLD EATERS INFANTRY or WORLD EATERS BIKER unit from your army that is not a CHAOS CULTIST is chosen to fight with. Until the end of that phase, that unit's Death to the False Emperor ability takes effect when targeting any enemy units, not just IMPERIUM units. In addition, when targeting IMPERIUM units, the ability takes effect on hit rolls of 5+.

2CP — BLOOD FOR THE BLOOD GOD!
World Eaters Stratagem
When blood rains, the warriors of the World Eaters are fearless.

Use this Stratagem in the Fight phase, after an enemy unit is destroyed as a result of an attack made by a WORLD EATERS model from your army. Until the start of your next turn, when a Morale test is taken for a friendly WORLD EATERS unit, do not roll the dice; it is automatically passed.

ARTEFACTS OF THE WORLD EATERS

If your army is led by a Chaos Space Marine Warlord, you can give one of these Artefacts of Chaos to a WORLD EATERS CHARACTER model from your army, instead of other Artefacts of Chaos presented elsewhere.

CRIMSON KILLER

This ornate pistol fires blasts of crimson plasma that crackle with murderous power and fierce energies that ignite body and soul alike. The bearer will oft follow up with a decapitating head strike and claim the singed skull for Khorne.

Model with plasma pistol only. This Relic replaces a plasma pistol and has the following profile:

WEAPON	RANGE	TYPE	S	AP	D
Crimson Killer	12"	Pistol 1	9	-3	3

Abilities: When resolving an attack made with this weapon, an unmodified wound roll of 4+ inflicts 1 mortal wound on the target in addition to any normal damage.

GOREFATHER

This immense chainaxe is said to have once been wielded by Angron himself. Though it was ultimately cast aside, this relic is of such immense importance to the Legion that wars have been fought between rival warbands seeking to claim it for themselves. One strong enough to wield Gorefather can scythe his enemies into scattering explosions of blood and ruined flesh.

Model with chainaxe only. This Relic replaces a chainaxe and has the following profile:

WEAPON	RANGE	TYPE	S	AP	D
Gorefather	Melee	Melee	+2	-2	3

Abilities: When resolving an attack made with this weapon, subtract 1 from the hit roll, and on an unmodified wound roll of 6 the target suffers 3 mortal wounds and the attack sequence ends.

BANNER OF RAGE

The Banner of Rage contains the bound souls of the most bloodthirsty of Khorne's servants. It radiates palpable waves of anger and an urge for slaughter that beat upon the minds of those nearby, driving them into a killing frenzy.

PRIEST model only. Once per battle, at the start of the Fight phase, a model with this Relic can unfurl the Banner of Rage. If they do, add 1 to the Attacks characteristic of models in friendly **WORLD EATERS** units whilst their unit is within 6" of that model.

BERSERKER GLAIVE

The bearer of this Daemon-infested killing tool is driven to a state of apoplectic frenzy by the proximity of its red-hot steel. His fellow World Eaters treat him with great caution, shunning him as a dangerous maniac even amongst his own bloodthirsty kind whilst venerating him as a living totem of rage. A host of Bloodletters are bound into the weapon's fabric, and by channelling the life essence of those it slays, the vampiric Daemon weapon ensures its isolated host can fight like a man possessed for weeks on end.

Model with power axe or axe of dismemberment only. This Relic replaces a power axe or axe of dismemberment and has the following profile:

WEAPON	RANGE	TYPE	S	AP	D
Berserker Glaive	Melee	Melee	+1	-2	2

Abilities: When the bearer would lose a wound, roll one D6; on a 5+ that wound is not lost.

HELM OF FURORE

The bearer of such a trophy is a champion that puts aside all concepts of loyalty. Only bloodshed and victorious combat matter. Within the helm a spiteful machine spirit lurks that stokes the bearer's butchers nails to even higher levels of frenzy, driving them further into the famed bloodlust that claims the sanity of the World Eaters.

INFANTRY model only. Add 2 to the Strength characteristic of a model with this Relic. At the start of your Charge phase, if a model with this Relic is within 8" of any enemy units, it must declare a charge.

BLOODHUNGER

Bloodhunger is a sentient suit of armour bonded with the wearer. This unholy union creates a mutual craving for red viscera harvested by battle. If indulged, armour and wearer alike heal grievous injuries and damage. When a champion of Khorne is linked with this unholy artefact and set loose into the midst of war, their symbiosis imbues them until there are no remaining adversaries to sake their thirst.

When an enemy model is destroyed in the Fight phase as a result of an attack made by a model with this Relic, roll one D6; on a 4+ the model with this Relic regains up to 1 lost wound.

WORLD EATERS TACTICAL OBJECTIVES

These Tactical Objectives are for use in Maelstrom of War missions to represent the strategies and tactics of the Legion on the battlefield.

If your army is led by a **WORLD EATERS** Warlord, these Tactical Objectives replace the Capture and Control Tactical Objectives (numbers 11-16) in the *Warhammer 40,000* rulebook. If a mission uses Tactical Objectives, players use the normal rules for using Tactical Objectives with the following exception: when a World Eaters player generates a Capture and Control objective (numbers 11-16), they instead generate the corresponding World Eaters Tactical Objective, as shown below. Other Tactical Objectives (numbers 21-66) are generated normally.

D66	TACTICAL OBJECTIVE
11	Kill Them Where They Stand
12	The Sacrament of Khorne
13	Skulls for the Skull Throne
14	Blood for the Blood God
15	Kill! Maim! Burn!
16	Bane of Sorcery

11 — KILL THEM WHERE THEY STAND

The enemy seeks to hold a strategic location against you. Show them the folly of their actions.

Score 1 victory point if an enemy unit that was controlling an objective marker at the start of your turn was destroyed as a result of an attack made by a **WORLD EATERS** model from your army this turn.

World Eaters

14 — BLOOD FOR THE BLOOD GOD

Khorne cares not from whence the blood flows, so long as it flows.

Score 1 victory point for each unit (friend or foe) that was destroyed as a result of an attack made with a melee weapon this turn (to a maximum of 6 victory points).

World Eaters

12 — SACRAMENT OF KHORNE

In the thick of the fighting, where his bloody work is done, Khorne's followers truly glorify their savage master.

Score 1 victory point if at least three **WORLD EATERS** units from your army made charge moves this turn.

World Eaters

15 — KILL! MAIM! BURN!

Kill! Maim! Burn! Kill! Maim! Burn! Kill! Maim! Burn! Kill! Maim! Burn! Kill! Maim! Burn! Kill! Maim! Burn! Kill! Maim! Burn! Kill! Maim! Burn! Kill! Maim! Burn!

Score 1 victory point if an enemy unit was destroyed as a result of an attack made by a **WORLD EATERS** model from your army in the Fight phase of this turn and that **WORLD EATERS** model's unit is still within 1" of an enemy unit at the end of the turn.

World Eaters

13 — SKULLS FOR THE SKULL THRONE

Khorne demands the skulls of the enemy's greatest champions.

Score D3 victory points if an enemy **CHARACTER** model was destroyed as a result of an attack made by a **WORLD EATERS** model from your army in the Fight phase of this turn.

World Eaters

16 — BANE OF SORCERY

Khorne despises little more than the cowardly use of sorcery.

Score D3 victory points if an enemy **PSYKER** model was destroyed as a result of an attack made by a **WORLD EATERS** model from your army this turn.

World Eaters

WORLD EATERS NAME GENERATOR

This section is a tool to help you forge a name for mighty warriors of your Legion to further build the background and personality of your army. If you wish to randomly generate a name for one of your World Eaters warriors, you can roll a D66 and consult the table below. To roll a D66, simply roll two D6, one after the other – the first represents tens, and the second represents digits, giving you a result between 11 and 66.

D66	NAME	D66	NAME
11	Khorgedd	11	Rex
12	Barask	12	the Destroyer
13	Brekh	13	Kharos
14	Griven	14	the Maimer
15	Nharax	15	the Blood-hungry
16	Ashkal	16	the Furious
21	Azkor	21	the Headsman
22	Orbak	22	Thaxxos
23	Garrek	23	Hakkan
24	Kreeg	24	the Reaper
25	Khaen	25	Rhugor
26	Sarvak	26	Korgath
31	Berek	31	Foe Ripper
32	Khrask	32	Zagoras
33	Davask	33	Spinehacker
34	Drakh	34	Skullfiend
35	Grosk	35	Redeye
36	Torgax	36	Damaskar
41	Varrak	41	Bloodgrin
42	Khargos	42	Axefist
43	Haska	43	Khorr
44	Rukh	44	Spinecrusher
45	Tarvakh	45	the Eightfold
46	Gharrax	46	the Blooded
51	Khoran	51	the Butcher
52	Azgorek	52	Khrul
53	Zagrek	53	Gorefist
54	Trosk	54	Bloodhair
55	Khorgor	55	the Cleaver
56	Oresk	56	Ghorum
61	Baska	61	Varren
62	Macer	62	Sykoth
63	Bhufor	63	Krassek
64	Sorkhos	64	Draxxigor
65	Larsakh	65	the Hound
66	Wrask	66	Eyegouger